All-American TRUCK STOPS

GUY KUDLEMYER & WAYNE HENDERSON

Iconografix

Iconografix
PO Box 446
Hudson, Wisconsin 54016 USA

Library of Congress Control Number: 2011936668

ISBN-13: 978-1-58388-286-3
ISBN-10: 1-58388-286-3

11 12 13 14 15 16 6 5 4 3 2 1

Printed in China

On the cover: The Lee Lewis Husky Truck Stop in Kalispell, Montana (top); the Cross Roads Shell Truck Stop in Park City, Kentucky (middle left); The Halfway House Truck Stop in Williamstown, Kentucky (middle right); Kenny's Truck Arena near Yankton, South Dakota (bottom left); and Streid's Standard Truck Stop in Bloomington, Illinois (bottom right). From coast-to-coast, the histories, evolutions, and stylistic developments of American Truck Stops and Travel Plazas are as varied as the customers that they serve.

BOOK PROPOSALS

Iconografix is a publishing company specializing in books for transportation enthusiasts. We publish in a number of different areas, including Automobiles, Auto Racing, Buses, Construction Equipment, Emergency Equipment, Farming Equipment, Railroads & Trucks. The Iconografix imprint is constantly growing and expanding into new subject areas.

Authors, editors, and knowledgeable enthusiasts in the field of transportation history are invited to contact the Editorial Department at Iconografix, Inc., PO Box 446, Hudson, WI 54016.

www.iconografixinc.com

TABLE OF CONTENTS

DEDICATION

This work is dedicated to my father Bill Kudlemyer, whose employment as a diesel mechanic for Chandler's Sand & Gravel in Palos Verdes, California, in my early years, started me down this road of fascination with everything trucking-related, and;

To my Mother Shirlee, whose tales of life on the road with her father, Elmer Salzman, who drove a truck for Republic Van Lines and allowed her travel with him occasionally, led to an interest in Little America, "The World's Largest Gas Station," and;

To Kristy, my wife, my life partner, my confidante, and chief source of both constructive criticism and continuous inspiration.

I love you all.
Guy Kudlemyer

I would like to thank my family for putting up with my intense interest all these years—to Mom and Dad, thanks for the little wooden Gulf sign that got all this started so long ago; and to Joanne and the kids for all of the day-to-day issues of living with a historian and collector. I would also like to thank everyone in the petroleum collectibles hobby for the information, the pictures, for every little nugget that makes it all possible.

Wayne Henderson

ACKNOWLEDGMENTS

Many people have contributed to this work either directly or indirectly, either by choice or by chance. It would be difficult to cite everyone who played a part in the construction process for this book. However, certain individual's efforts deserve to be noted. Among them:

Jessica Rowcroft, whose Historical Preservation Thesis at Cornell University, "The Truck Stop Industry in The United States" resulted in the definition of the Four Generations of truck stop constructions cited and used heavily in this book; it is the interpretations of these Four Generations upon which a good deal of the text in this book is based. Ms. Rowcroft was kind enough to email me a copy of that Thesis many years ago, which planted the seed in my head to write this book.

Authors *Scott Benjamin* and *Wayne Henderson,* whose numerous petroleum and petroliana-related books were heavily leaned upon in various sections of this work, especially where information was required concerning various oil companies' histories.

Jerry Keyser of *Check The Oil!* magazine, who is always willing to publish any petroleum or petroliana-related article that happens to fall out of my Macintosh. Without the success of having magazine articles printed in his magazine (and others), I might not have had the temerity to think that I could get a book printed.

Fred Probst of Clay Center Kansas, who cheerfully shared many insightful trucking and truck stop anecdotes, and who continually offers encouragement for any of my trucking, truck stop, or petroliana-related editorial endeavors.

Earl Ma of Honolulu, Hawaii, who, before his unfortunate passing his late 20s in 2005, was generally regarded in the petroliana hobby as the reigning "expert" of all things UNION 76, and Blue & White Truck Stops-related, and who graciously granted me the opportunity to benefit from his extensive research of the Blue & White truck stop brand and chain. Thank you, Earl, and, "Aloha."

Jessica Breitbach, whose Columbia University Masters Thesis, "A Home Away From Home: Telling The Story of The Trucking Industry Through the Preservation of 1960s Truck Stops" provided insights into truck stop conditions during that period. My meager participation in the preparation of her Thesis (answering general questions about truck stops and the loaning of truck stop-related materials) resulted in the receipt of my very own bound copy of the Thesis, upon which I drew in several sections of this work.

Gary Brewer of Indianapolis, Indiana, who readily shared any and all of his personal truck stop photos (Blue & White Truck Stops and otherwise), and whose emails concerning truck stops kept me itchin' to get this work completed.

The too-numerous-to-mention Internet cruddy buddies who willingly supplied scanned images of truck stop photos and postcards that they had collected, whenever I asked. For you guys, all I can say is: "The work was hard, but the pay is low."

And, last but not least, my publisher, *Iconografix,* of Hudson, Wisconsin, and specifically, Editorial Director *Dylan Frautschi,* who took the chance that we all might actually be able to make ourselves some money by publishing this ragged agglomeration of data.

To everyone mentioned above, I am most gratefully indebted.

(Oh yeah... Let me not forget Tom T. Hall and *"Ravishing Ruby"*...)

Guy Kudlemyer
Thurston, Oregon
June, 2011

PREFACE

As an author, I'm often asked by the curious, "So, how long does it take to write a book?" I used to reply, "I don't know." It was true; I *didn't* know. I didn't know because, prior to now, I'd only been a magazine articles author. So, I wasn't lying.

"Oh, that has to be a lie. You're an author, right? So, how long does it take? Really. How long?"

Despite the book that you are now holding in your hands, I can still honestly reply, "I don't know." I don't know because the book you are currently reading isn't finished yet. No matter how thorough one intends to be in one's writings, there's always *one more thing I should have included.* And then another, and another, as the thought process continues its expansion. But by now, it's too late; the publisher has your manuscript, and they are doing the exact *opposite* to it what you'd like to be doing to it: They're "editing" it (read: cutting things out), and you want to be adding to it.

I can give you a rough guess though, based on this, my first (and thus far only) foray into book writing territory: It takes more than 40 years to write a book. Yes, you read correctly: *40 years.*

The seed for this book was planted when I was 12 years old; the summer of 1968. I had just returned from a family cross-country vacation trip of approximately 5,000 miles. From the Lincoln Highway and Route 66 two-lanes, to the still-to-be completed four-lanes of I-15, I-40, I-44, I-55, and I-80, I saw more truck stops and gas stations than I ever had before in my young life; an event that allowed me to learn the various oil company brands that were the most active in various parts of the country. I was even lucky enough to be able to stop at a few truck stops here and there along the way when the trusty 1968 Mercury station wagon that we were riding in needed to eat. The idea of spending one's life on the road became an intriguing one to me during this trip, and becoming a trucker seemed like an ideal way to get paid for doing something you love; a sure secret to success. Learning the rudiments of drafting in my junior high school drafting and drawing classes allowed my colored pencils to begin to semi-adequately depict memories of truck stops seen or visited along the road during that trip, in the privacy of my bedroom at home; therein, the "seed."

The location of our residence only compounded the situation: We lived across the street from the company that employed my father; a company named "Chandler's Sand & Gravel" (headed by "Old Man Chandler") that ran nearly 100 trucks past our house at all hours of the day and night, allowing me to learn the various makes and models of trucks in production at that time. My father fostered my burgeoning interest in the trucking industry by graciously taking whatever time was necessary to talk with me about trucks and to answer all of my silly questions. In addition, he bankrolled several excursions to various Los Angeles area truck dealerships in that same Mercury station wagon, always providing a tasty luncheon of hot dogs or tamales. During these excursions, my sticky hands voraciously hauled off many of the dealerships' expensive, four-color-process sales materials by the dozens, which I three-hole punched and placed into three ring binders for safekeeping (most of which I still have). My poor dad endured many embarrassing moments, I'm sure, as his indelicate offspring ran willy-nilly through truck showrooms and around sales lots, jumping up and down on, and climbing into every truck on the premises.

As time went on, my urge to become a trucker waned, but the seed idea of documenting trucks and truck stops began to blossom after the completion of a degree in Graphic Design and Publishing from the University of Oregon, in Eugene. Working for various Graphic Design firms and book/magazine publishers thereafter allowed me access to trucking-related and petroleum-related publishing industry people. These folks were able to start me on my way towards my eventual goal of writing a truck stop-related book by publishing some of my burgeoning initial works.

So, what did I think of to include after this manuscript went to Iconografix? Well, there was that shot of that GULF truck stop down in Florida. And a photo of the "Mass 10" Getty truck stop up in Massachusetts. One of my internet correspondents just emailed me a shot of a P-I-E Peterbilt fueling at Little America in the early 1950s… To research those will take me a few more hours, so I guess the completion of this book is still out there a bit. I'm *really* not lying: I'm still not sure how long it takes to write a book. But I sincerely hope you enjoy the partially completed work that follows…

INTRODUCTION

A common definition of a truck stop might be: "A roadside commercial enterprise dedicated to the provision of services to a long-haul truck and its driver."

The earliest truck stops, dating from the 1920s or so, offered limited services for both truck and driver. For the truck, perhaps fuel and oil. For the driver, perhaps sandwiches or a lunch counter. Most "truck stops" were simply gas stations located on major roads between towns or cities. Because most "long-hauls" were simple inter-city runs between local towns over crude graveled roads, not much more was necessary; not even diesel fuel (until the 1950s). Early trucks ran on hard-rubber tires; when later trucks adopted pneumatic tires, perhaps tire repair service might become available. As there was no coast-to-coast trucking until well into the 1930s, there was no need to consider supplying sleeping facilities for drivers, and no need to be open 24 hours a day.

Fifty-plus years later, in the late 1970s, the truck stop's current incarnation, the "Travel Plaza," was born. Now not only catering to truckers, but (again) to auto travelers as well, the list of provisions and services has increased exponentially since then: fuels, oils, lubricants; maintenance and repair facilities; truck washing facilities; tire repair facilities; overnight parking for big rigs; road and towing services; truck replacement parts and accessories; a restaurant (often offering a buffet smorgasbord); a motel; showering facilities for truckers; communication facilities (bulletin boards/telephones/internet); barbering and dentistry facilities; a chapel; a video game room; a mini-movie theater featuring late-run movies on DVD and a couple hundred cable channels; fast-food restaurants and ice cream/donut/cinnamon roll emporiums; a souvenir shop; and toilets and restroom facilities.

But… *There was a time when a truck stop actually catered primarily to truckers, and it occurred during the intervening years between these two auto-focused extremes, and it is what constitutes the bulk of the interesting history of the development of the truck stop.* The pages that follow are an attempt to chronicle some of the more significant events and critical developments during the evolution of the truck stop.

This treatise is focused primarily the evolution of the truck stop in the U.S.; secondarily, it supplies a limited amount of information concerning truck stops in Canada. Perspectives of truck stops in countries outside of North America are outside the scope of this book.

We had a ball being in the driver's seat for the compilation of this publication. If you are the least bit interested in the evolution of the North American truck stop, then jump into the passenger seat and sit with us as we shift our gears through the chapters on this past-to-present run. We'll pull our rig into some of the most prominent information stopovers on the truck stop information highway time-line, and delineate the roads we traveled to arrive at our destination. It will be a fascinating haul!

(Any comments, omissions, errors, discussions, or updates on any of the following texts, should be directed to Guy Kudlemyer at RetroTruckStops@comcast.net, or Wayne Henderson at pcmpublishing@triad.rr.com)

In 1935, Hickok Oil Co. opened one of their Hi-Speed service gas stations at the intersection of Michigan routes 53 and 21 in Imlay City, Michigan. The dealer incorporated a restaurant into the station and began operating on a 24-hour basis, promoting his station as a good stopping point for trucks. This simple facility is, as best as can be determined, the first service station in the country to market itself as a "truck stop." This photo shows the station shortly after it opened. The pylon tower was a feature of Hi-Speed stations from the 1930s until the brand was replaced by the PURE brand name in 1951.

Chapter 1
PRE-INTERSTATE HIGHWAY AMERICA

At the turn of the 20th Century, the highway system criss-crossing the U.S. was a haphazard network of local farm-to-market roads that were not designed for, nor intended to, support long-distance highway travel. The Federal-Aid Road Act of 1916, signed by U.S. President Woodrow Wilson, began the gradual improvement of the U.S. highway system. Unfortunately, improvement progressed in a chaotic and uneven pace; even though the Federal government supplied the funding for road development in each state, there was no Federal management of the various states' road-building programs, nor any offering of design or planning assistance to the individual states.

The subsequent Federal Highway Act of 1921 made an effort to remedy this oversight. With this Act, only certain roads specifically designed for interstate or intercounty traffic were approved for Federal monetary assistance. The signing of this Act was designed to eliminate the all-too-common occurrence of drastically changing road quality at county or state lines.

In Germany, during the time of the signing of the Federal Highway Act of 1921, Rudolf Diesel was perfecting an invention for which he had received a patent in the mid to late 1890s—the Diesel engine. An American, Clessie Cummins, took interest in this new, non-spark ignited engine, and began experimenting. America's first diesel-powered vehicle took to the road on Christmas Day, 1929 in Indiana. On March 20, 1930, Clessie Cummins proved the viability of this engine by establishing a new world's speed record for a diesel-powered vehicle of 80.4 mph. Within little more than a decade from this milestone, the diesel engine would begin its ascendancy as the engine of choice for long-haul trucking.

Today's Interstate Highway System was still decades into the future at the point of Cummins' achievement and had not yet been envisioned by anyone in Washington who possessed the power to start the political wheels turning that would be necessary to eventuate its inception. But a seminal event had occurred a little more than a decade before Clessie Cummins had so convincingly brought the diesel engine's viability to the forefront of collected vehicular consciousness as a serious challenger to the gasoline engine's contemporary predominance.

EISENHOWER, THE AUTOBAHN, AND THE INTERSTATE HIGHWAY SYSTEM

Truck manufacturer GMC was ostensibly the first to attempt to demonstrate that coast-to-coast truck travel was possible. Behind the wheel of a 1916 GMC 1-1/2 ton truck sat William Warwick; beside him sat his wife. Under oath to keep the truck moving with no acceptance of offers of assistance, the Warwicks completed GMC's planned Seattle-to-New York-to-Seattle round trip in only 68 days; an amazing feat for the time.

In 1919, Lt. Col. Dwight D. Eisenhower embarked on a 62-day trek as a member of the U.S. Army's first attempt to move men, trucks, machinery, and artillery via a transcontinental convoy. The only transcontinental avenue available at the time was the newly-established Lincoln Highway. The Highway's "graveled at best, mud-bog at worst," loose interconnection of existing roads was punctuated by inadequate bridges, inadequate fueling and respite facilities, and inadequate signage. Arriving at the terminus of the trek was not so easy.

Getting lost *was* easy, as was having a heavily-laden truck destroy a bridge, instantly halting progress of the following trucks until a new bridge could be built.

Eisenhower's later stint as commander of the Allied Expeditionary Force in Germany in the early 1940s during WWII gave him an idea that would enhance the movement of people, cargo, and military armaments within the U.S.—to establish a network of Federally-funded improved roads. The now-General Eisenhower had easily moved personnel, trucks, and equipment on the expansive German autobahn network during WWII. When he returned to the U.S. after the war, much of the country's road network had been paved, but was still only two lanes, one in each direction. A system of roads sporting two lanes in each direction would allow for increased traffic capacity, as well as a passing lane to keep slower traffic, such as trucks, from impeding traffic flow.

As U.S. President, Eisenhower's June 29, 1956 signing of *The Federal-Aid Highway Act of 1956* gave birth to the *Dwight D. Eisenhower National System of Interstate and Defense Highways*—what we commonly refer to today as the "Interstates."

GAS STATIONS BEGET TRUCK STOPS

Historians generally agree that the gas station, as an architecturally-established building type, had its beginnings in 1905 in St. Louis, Missouri. C. H. Laessig, proprietor of the Automobile Gasoline Co., attached a garden hose and faucet to an old water heater tank and sold gasoline to motorists at a gasoline bulk storage facility outside of town. Sylvanus F. Bowser, operating independently from Laessig in St. Louis, adapted one of his earlier inventions—a well pump—to pump kerosene and gasoline from a remote tank and began marketing the new apparatus in 1905 as a "Filling Station."

In 1907, The Standard Oil Co. of California created an off-street site in Seattle for fueling autos utilizing a device similar to Laessig's—a hose and nozzle attached to an elevated storage tank. This is often cited as America's first "filling station" because the site itself was specifically created for the purpose, even though it also operated as a gasoline bulk storage facility. Laessig's follow-up 1909 effort in St. Louis is often cited as the "first" gas station because it was conceived and operated as a facility that was separate from a bulk storage plant, unlike Standard's. The Gulf Oil Co. of Pittsburgh, Pennsylvania, took the auto-fueling idea to the next level in 1913 when they built the first off-street facility specifically designed and constructed for the purpose of fueling autos, in Pittsburgh, in 1913, using pumps that were genealogically linked to Bowser's 1905 prototype; this was the de facto "first" gas station.

The PURE Oil Co. had purchased a controlling interest in Hickok Oil Company in 1928, but made no effort to rebrand the operation until after the remaining portion of the company had been purchased in 1951. Hickok Oil had marketed under the Hi-Speed name since 1917 and had developed an extensive network of stations in Ohio and Michigan, with many locations featuring an elaborate pylon tower entranceway. After PURE replaced the Hi-Speed brand in the early 1950s, the Hi-Speed name on the buildings' pylons were replaced with "PURE" spelled out in bright blue neon. The original truck stop at Imlay City, Michigan, was no exception, and in this mid-1950s photo we see the building remodeled and re-imaged to the PURE brand.

As the gas station evolved, a splinter type—the truck stop—followed closely behind.

The need for a separate facility to service trucks had not yet been isolated at the gas station's birth. Trucks themselves were often simply converted Model T's. Some simply sported a flatbed behind the driver, while others were more extensively modified to allow for the pulling of a trailer. Several companies offered springs and frame-modifying kits to assist in the transformation of a standard Model T to a vehicle with higher load-carrying capacity. Henry Ford himself teamed with trailer manufacturer August Fruehauf in 1914 to create the Ford Model TT, which many consider to be Ford's first actual "truck."

However, as late as 1912, most trucks, whatever their configuration, rarely traveled more than 25 to 50 miles from their home location. For long-distance transportation of goods, the railroads were still dominant; trucks served simply as feeders to the railways. That had changed substantially by the 1930s, when innovations such as a driver-protecting enclosed cab, pneumatic tires, and an ever-increasing number of paved highway miles, allowed trucks to compete with the slow and often unpredictable railroads on short intercity runs. It was at this point that the truck stop, as a separate automotive vehicular facility had its beginnings.

TRUCK STOPS DIVERGE FROM THEIR GAS STATION ROOTS

In their earliest incarnation, truck stops varied little from their gas station parentage, and were not even designated as such. Early gas station operators seeking increased trade helped to establish the truck stop as a separate roadside business type. Many times, these stations were operated by farmers who owned large plots of land with road frontage; the low maneuverability of trucks required these large land parcels for fueling and parking activities. Dad pumped fuels and made minor repairs, Mom and Sis served up sandwiches in the kitchen (as well as fresh fruit from the farm's orchards), and Junior washed windshields and cleaned headlights. These "Mom & Pop" facilities comprised the very first truck stops.

In the early 1930s, the number of truck drivers increased from approximately 1 million to approximately 3.1 million. Sensing a burgeoning market share, the Hickok Oil Company of Toledo, Ohio, which marketed under the Hi-Speed trademark, responded with the world's first "built from the ground up" truck stop in 1935, constructed at a cost of $40,000. It was located in Imlay City, Michigan, at the intersection of Michigan Highways 21 and 53.

During the 1940s and into the '50s, the truck stop as a gas station sub-type progressed steadily from its

In the early 1960s, the Imlay City, Michigan, PURE truck stop was remodeled again and the pylon tower, a feature since its opening in 1935, was eliminated. In this 1960 photo, the facility resembles the then-current image for conventional PURE service stations. The station survived at least through the 1970 rebranding to the UNION 76 brand.

Hickok/Hi-Speed, Imlay City beginnings to become an American roadside archetype. The truck stop concept originated by Hickok was advanced primarily by the development and the adoption of the diesel as the engine of choice for long-haul trucking. The increased load-pulling efficiency and greater fuel economy offered by the diesel made for an easy adoption for situations where heavy cargo carrying capacity at higher speeds was a necessity.

Hickok Oil had been owned in part by the PURE Oil Company since 1928. In 1951 the purchase was completed and the Hi-Speed chain was rebranded to PURE. From the time of the founding of Hi-Speed in 1917 in Toledo by A. S. Hickok, until the PURE Oil Company's purchase of all 2,000 of Hi-Speed's outlets in Ohio and Michigan, the truck stop had been birthed and had grown to adolescence. It was the continued hands-on involvement by large oil companies, coupled with a monumental, nationwide, interstate road-building project that was the precursor for the demise of the "Mom & Pop" truck stop.

"MOM & POPS" GIVE WAY TO OIL COMPANY TRUCK STOPS

The coming of the Interstates spawned a whole new breed of truck stop—one that was no longer fronted on a two-lane, but instead was sited at strategic entrances to and exits from limited-access, four-lane, high speed Interstate Highways. Oil com-

A better photo showing the newly remodeled Imlay City facility in about 1960.

panies, such as The PURE Oil Co., headquartered in Illinois, the Skelly Oil Co. of Kansas City, Missouri, and the various incarnations of the Standard Oil Co., possessed the resources needed to take on a systematic plan of action to replace aging two-lane properties with gleaming new glass and porcelain-enameled Interstate Highway truck stop palaces.

At the point when President Eisenhower signed *The Federal-Aid Highway Act* in 1956, virtually all

Simmons Terminal takes its place as one of America's first truck stops, alongside several other facilities showcased in this work. In the spring of 1935, Simmons Oil Co. signed on as the Cities Service distributor for South Hill, Virginia, and the surrounding countryside. Simmons' base of operations was a service station and truck terminal on U.S. 1, just south of South Hill. Sometime before 1938, Simmons Oil became Parker Oil Co., and the reorganized company began selling PURE products for their region. The older photo here shows Simmons' Terminal while it was branded Cities Service. As the concept of the truck stop evolved, the facility was remodeled and enlarged. When PURE rebranded the Hi-Speed operation and began exploring the possibilities of expanding their truck stop network, they studied the operation of Simmons Terminal, which had functioned as a PURE branded truck stop since the mid-1930s. The later photo shows the facility as it appeared in the early 1950s, with its elaborate neon PURE sign along the roadside. After Interstate 85 bypassed this location, a new Simmons Terminal was built along the new routing, although this location continued to function as a truck stop for a few more years. Today, this location serves as the offices for Parker Oil Co. and one of their Red Barn Convenience Stores.

of the truck stops in the U.S. fronted two-lane highways. By the mid-1960s, new truck stop construction was centered nearly 100% on new, Interstate Highway locations; by 1969, there were more than 2,000 truck stops operating in the U.S.

PURE's 1957 truck stop network total of 168 locations in 20 states, stretching from Dunseith, North Dakota, to Florida City, Florida, had expanded to 295 locations in 28 states by 1969, with almost all of the new constructions by then occurring on the new Interstate routes. As the Interstate Highways were completed, PURE's truck stop totals grew from 168 outlets in 1957, to 295 in 1969, when the Union Oil Co. of California assimilated the PURE Oil Co. and rebranded the locations to its 76 brand.

Similarly, Skelly's totals increased from as few as 40 truck stop locations in 14 midwestern states stretching from Colorado to Louisiana in 1958, to 217 in 1975. Again, totals increased concomitantly with the expansion of the Interstate Highway System.

The farmer-operated and Mom & Pop truck stops left behind on the back roads and pre-Interstate two-lanes were forced to either close their doors with the decline in business as traffic shifted to the Interstates, or to find creative ways to compete with the corporate-funded, multi-million dollar highway manors out on the four-lane.

DIFFERENCES PROVIDE SHARP CONTRASTS BETWEEN "MOM & POP" AND BIG OIL

The dichotomy was stark: On the two-lane, Mom & Pop offered a converted pitched-roof clapboard farmhouse for a makeshift café, handmade signage nailed to outside building walls; a couple of globe-topped 1940s-era fuel pumps out front; restrictive parking facilities; sandwiches, or hamburgers and fries, at a multi-stooled luncheon counter; gang showers and dormitory-style sleeping facilities (where available); a pay phone perhaps; and gravel or dirt approaches and exits.

Out on the Interstate, Big Oil offered the latest in 1960s modern architecture, featuring flat-topped glass and steel structures; full-service restaurants with all-you-can-eat buffets; ticket-imprinting fuel pumps; expansive multi-acre asphalt-paved parking; garage and mechanic services; individual room sleeping facilities; a convenience store; wire services for contacting brokers concerning available loads; Western Union telegraph services; "Instant Check" and "Com-Check" services to supply truckers with money while on the road; and a TV lounge. Some even offered a truckers' store, stocked to the ceiling with clothing, footwear, snacks, magazines, pharmaceuticals, truck accessories, and a barber shop.

There were similar contrasts in primary and sec-

In the late 1960s, Interstate 85 bypassed the section of U.S. 1 where the original Simmons Terminal was located. A new Simmons Terminal was developed along the new route, located at the only exit between South Hill, Virginia, and the North Carolina state line. It remains in operation today, although enlarged and modernized from its appearance in this 1969 photo.

ondary site signage between Mom & Pop and Big Oil. "Primary" signage (typically the oil company's logo or the name of the oil company spelled out, sometimes including the truck stop's name or the price of diesel fuel) is placed in a near-haphazard fashion at a Mom & Pop truck stop, with no standardization in location from truck stop to truck stop, other than a porcelain-enamel or backlit plastic roadside sign along the two-lane. Often, but not always, primary signage was placed atop the building; sometimes, it was on a canopy over the fuel islands; in some instances, it could simply be a homemade sandwich-board sign facing the roadway.

On the other hand, Big Oil truck stops mandated standardized signage construction and placement for each company-constructed outlet. Usually, the logo or spelled-out oil company name was placed prominently atop the main building, along with a generic RESTAURANT sign, generally over the main entrance, or sometimes integrated into the design of the building itself; an oil company logo sign, sometimes

In addition to the South Hill location, Simmons Terminals opened a truck stop on U.S. 301 south of Emporia, Virginia, just north of the North Carolina state line. With the two companion locations, Simmons Terminals service was available to most of the north-south trucking along the East Coast. This photo was taken in April of 1953. Although bypassed by Interstate 95 in 1959, an exit serves this location and Simmons Terminal Emporia remains in operation today. Another Simmons location operated in Keysville, Virginia.

Another Peggy Ann restaurant was built in the late 1930s in Somerset, Kentucky. Again, TEXACO products were sold, and the location served as a Greyhound rest stop and fuel facility. The original photo here dates from before WWII, the later one, where Standard Oil products were being sold, dates from the late 1940s or early 1950s.

A third Peggy Ann location was built in the mid-1930s in Burnside, Kentucky, on U.S. 27. TEXACO products and official status as a Greyhound rest stop were also found at Burnside. Very little is known about this location beyond what can be discerned from the photo.

The Peggy Ann truck stop operation was perhaps the first truck stop chain. Very little has been discovered about the origins of the operation, but early photos indicate origins around 1937 or 1938. The operation began as a roadside hotel and café on U.S. 27-70 in Rockwood, Tennessee. Rooms were available for tourists, and the restaurant was an official meal stop for the Greyhound Bus Lines. The two early photos indicate that TEXACO products were then being sold at that time. In later years, an addition on the front of the original building enlarged the restaurant and added a 1950s modern Shell station. The later photo dates from the early 1960s. The Peggy Ann continued in operation until at least the 1970s.

towering six stories or more to allow travelers cruising at 70 mph plenty of time to make the decision to stop, was found along the Interstate roadside, often including the words, "Truck Stop" and/or the price of diesel fuel. All signage was factory-produced.

Likewise, "Secondary" signage (adjunct signage typified by its smaller size) is placed in an even more random fashion at Mom & Pop Truck Stops; typically these signs would advertise, "free parking"; "Café;" a particular brand of oil sold; Coca-Cola; Pepsi; trailer refrigeration repair service; or even a short list of available menu items (with prices) at the RESTAURANT (that nearly always specialized in "Home Cooking"), and could be placed at roadside, atop the converted farmhouse café, on the fuel pump islands, on powerline or telephone poles, or at any other convenient place where a sandwich-board sign could be placed out of harm's way. More often than not, most of the primary and secondary signage at a Mom & Pop stop was handmade, either by the owners themselves, or, if the truck stop was particularly successful, perhaps by a local professional sign painter.

Secondary signage at truck stops constructed by Big Oil were generally fewer in number, or, in extreme instances, altogether non-existent. Where these signs *were* extant, Big Oil placed the same emphasis on standardization in construction and placement for this secondary signage as they had mandated for signage of the primary variety.

Paved asphalt parking came increasingly into use during this time, and became a necessity for new oil company truck stop constructions. It was considered to be an expensive undertaking, being a free amenity from which there is no direct monetary return. However, indirectly, paved parking was a drawing card that might help to entice a driver to choose an oil company truck stop with a tasty all-you-can-eat buffet over a Mom & Pop facility, where he might have to slog through mud, or contend with dusty conditions while making his way to a luncheon counter for a cold-cut sandwich and potato chips.

In an effort to increase security and to assist in ease of parking, parking lots at new oil company truck stop constructions universally featured fluorescent lighting. Mom & Pop truck stops offered little parking lot lighting, if any at all, and almost always of the incandescent variety, which offers lesser capabilities for flooding large land expanses.

Mom & Pop truck stops generally tended to have ancillary truck services separated from driver services, and housed in separate buildings: Fuel islands and café were at roadside; parking, restrooms, and repair services, if available, were shunted to the rear. At oil company truck stops constructed in the '60s, all services were designed into a single building. When they *were* necessary, most ancillary buildings were situated away from easy view from the road, behind, but still within reach of, the main building.

As early as 1960, the PURE Oil Co., in an early edition of their booklet-style truck stop directories, declared, "Pure Oil TruckStops have been designed from the ground up to serve the every need of the modern over-the-road trucker and his equipment. In developing these TruckStops, Pure Oil's aim has been that 'Nothing is too good for the trucker', and the TruckStops shown here are the fulfillment of this motto. The stations that make up this chain not only represent the finest in facilities, but each is well stocked with 'Truck-Tested' products."

In 1965, Jerry Sanner, General Manager—Truck Industry Sales for PURE, used a platform in the center-spread of that year's PURE Truck Stop Directory to banner that, "Things Are Getting Better All The Time." He followed with a note aimed directly at his trucker customer: "There is a great deal of personal satisfaction in seeing the way you fellows react to our program. I have spent over 30 years of my life trying to upgrade over-the-road truckstops for drivers. Sometimes I have been criticized for making things too plush or fancy. But these critics have had to eat their words every time. Now, instead of wall-to-wall concrete, you are getting wall-to-wall carpeting and private baths. Now, instead of hash houses, you have fine food in pleasant surroundings."

TRUCK STOPS BECOME "TRAVEL PLAZAS"

As with nearly everything else in the U.S., bigger is usually better, and so it goes with the truck stop. Perhaps Osborne Jay Call, founder of the Flying J chain said it best, with the building of the first Flying J "travel plaza" in Ogden, Utah, in 1979: "We built the stop having in mind dealing with people, not servicing trucks." While not having originated the people-servicing idea, Jay was obviously attempting to take credit for its exponential expansion in the truck stop market.

In "The Flying J Story," author Howard M. Carlisle notes that the construction of the first Flying J "travel plaza" was to offer, "…generous parking (including overnight); service islands separating trucks from cars; tiled bathrooms and showers; attractive interior and exterior; a television lounge and rest area; ample telephones at strategic locations; and restaurant facilities at least the equal of national franchised chains." Mom & Pop's sandwiches and potato chips served on a stool at a counter back on the old two-lane clearly was no longer adequate.

Older truck stops could sometimes successfully respond to this assault by adding services to their existing architecture, as well as by updating their roadside signage. But their days were numbered nonetheless,

Penfield's Windy Acres was one of the earliest truck stops in Minnesota. Located on U.S. 52 just south of Cannon Falls, the original facility consisted of a Webb branded service station with a small café. Repair facilities and a motel were added within a few years, and other truckers' services followed. In the mid-1950s fuel supply was switched from Webb to W. H. Barber's Mee-te-or brand. After PURE purchased W. H. Barber, the facility was enlarged and entered into the PURE Truck Stop network. In 1991, the main building was remodeled for service as an antique mall, which remains in operation today. The oldest photos here date from about 1952; the Mee-te-or photos from about 1955; and the PURE brand photos from about 1960.

as the bulk of the traffic shifted to the seamless, "no stop-light coast-to-coast" Interstates.

Today's Interstate Highway travel plazas are an even further cry from the original Mom & Pop tuck stop, and typically feature an expanded list of truck stop services that goes beyond even what Jerry Sanner's PURE outlets of the 1960s, and Osborne Jay Call's Flying J outlets of 1979 had offered. Often, today's trucker will find the following: franchised chain eateries (such as Subway, Taco Bell, Popeye's Fried Chicken, and the like) in addition to full-service restaurants and/or buffets; truck weigh scales; convenience stores; Permit Services; Emergency Road Service; barber shops and beauty salons; medical and dental clinics; high-speed internet; and houses of worship with chapel services. In the early 2000s, TravelCenters of America (T/A) built a prototype truck stop in Commerce City, Colorado, that took designing cues from such unlikely sources as the swanky Ritz-Carlton hotel chain and features marbled tile in the restrooms. This "from the ground-up" re-design served as the flagship for an eventual complete makeover of all of the T/A properties.

At the Giant Travel Center near Gallup, New Mexico, diners in the 300-seat restaurant can choose from coffee or lattés, biscuits and gravy, or chicken breasts in mango sauce, all while comfortably seated in cozy ambience with a faux wood-burning fireplace as its centerpiece.

Portland Oregon's Jubitz Travel Center features a

four-story, 100-room Portlander Inn motel, a video arcade, an 80 seat movie theater featuring first-run movies, lottery services, a medical center, a hair salon, a chiropractor, a country-western lounge with two dance floors, shoe repair, and coin-op and drop-off laundry services.

But the transition from truck stop to travel plaza, while popular with auto tourists, was not necessarily wholly embraced by the trucking fraternity. One trucker from the period put it thus: "When UNION 76 took over PURE, their new logo upset a lot of drivers. It went from a 'PURE Truck Stop' to a 'UNION 76 Auto/Truck Stop.' Not only did truckers get second billing, but 76 was now inviting the tourist to stop in. A truck stop was a haven for the trucker, offering a brief period where he could get away from the 4-wheelers and tourists, and now 76 was inviting them into their sanctuary. They did provide a separate dining and lounge area for the drivers, but it wasn't the same. Now instead of 'Truck Stop,' a lot of places are calling themselves 'Travel Stops' and 'Travel Centers,' dropping the word 'Truck' altogether."

With the coming of the Interstate Highway System, the formerly nearly transparent world of the two-lane truckers' Mom & Pop stop-overs was quickly coming into public view. What had previously been categorized as greasy-spoon coffee dungeons populated by shiftless, chain-smoking diesel cowboys was now beginning to be perceived as sparkling highway oases where travelers of all persuasions were courted. Dad, Mom, and the kids could shut down the family station wagon at the gas pump within sight of the fueling diesel dragons and feel comfortable ambling inside for a quick restroom stop, or a delicious buffet lunch.

During the 1970s, the upscaling trend ran unabated despite the OPEC-induced "energy crisis." Although gasoline sales were down due to higher costs and more limited availabilities, truck traffic and associated fuel sales surged as trucks continued to displace railroads for freight deliveries; more truck stops and "travel plazas" were built, with each becoming more elaborate than the one before.

PRE-TRAVEL PLAZA TRUCK STOP TYPOLOGIES

In a treatise entitled, "The Truck Stop Industry in the United States," noted historical preservationist Jessica Rowcroft breaks down the evolution of the truck stop into four major types, and several sub-types. The typologies Rowcroft proffers are the product of extensive research, investigation, and analysis during the late 1990s. The four major types and their reliant sub-types will be paraphrased and outlined below, and the compulsory categorization of historically-significant truck stops referred to in this text will adhere to Rowcroft's categorizations:

FIRST GENERATION TRUCK STOPS

• Beginning as early as 1925 and lasting until as late as the early 1950s; individually owned and operated, Mom & Pop-operated stops.

• Usually consisting of reconfigured existing buildings (most often a farmhouse), with a minimal number of purpose-built structures.

• Typically located on the perimeters of large towns or cities, almost always directly on intercity, two-lane routes.

• Many stops open 24 hours per day, seven days per week.

• Café, fueling facilities, mechanical repair, and some limited dormitory-style sleeping facilities were among some of the meager services sometimes being offered.

• Parking and fueling areas paved in gravel or dirt.

TRIPLE "O" TRUCKSTOP
ROUTE 421, LODI, OHIO

Donald S. Grimm operated the Triple "O" Truck Stop (#160) located on Highway 42 in Lodi, Ohio, in the early 1960s. By 1967, this location had undergone a major makeover that gave it a very Wildwood-like appearance, and had become PURE Truck Stop #195. This early 1960s shot shows the fuel island building, with service building behind at left, and the restaurant at right-center. A late 1950s White conventional can be seen fueling. Note the uniquely-shaped Triple "O" signage at roadside. This outlet was converted to PURE from Atlantic in the early 1960s, and it can be seen as an Atlantic branded location elsewhere in this book.

U.S. Highway 29 through Virginia is located on the eastern slope of the Blue Ridge Mountains and is one of the most scenic highways in the eastern United States. North of Charlottesville, the 29 Truck Stop operated for many years. TEXACO products were sold here when this photo was taken, in about 1952, shortly before they rebranded to PURE and became part of the PURE Truck Stop network. It is seen elsewhere in this book under the PURE branding.

Headed south out of Savannah, Georgia, on U.S. 17, truckers were confronted with a number of choices when it came to truck stops. One of the stops along the way was the Seminole Truck Terminal, which advertised itself as the "largest drive-in on the Coastal Highway." Evidently this claim must relate to lot size, as the actual facilities appear to be relatively small. A diner can be seen at the far left, with a bunkhouse at the center of the lot, and a fuel station to the right. No particular oil company brand is evident. It is seen here as it was in the late 1940s.

• Rectangular-shaped, shallow lots with maximum roadside frontage.

• Allowed for mixed-traffic (auto and truck) usage, with no separation of parking or access to facilities

• Catered to both auto and truck traffic, but with the emphasis on trucks.

SECOND GENERATION TRUCK STOPS

• Beginning as early as the mid-1940s, as a response to the increase in truck traffic and of skilled truck driver labor at the end of WWII.

• Still mostly Mom & Pop-operated facilities.

• Approaches and parking still gravel and/or dirt.

• Consisted of multiple building types situated on larger lots, but with no particular uniformly-applied configuration.

• Increasing adoption of the diesel engine now required that both gasoline and diesel fuels be offered for sale.

• By the late 1950s, large petroleum companies began to make sizeable investments in the burgeoning truck stop industry; this interest was further bolstered by the 1956 signing of the *Federal-Aid Highway Act of 1956*, which gave birth to the Interstates, and created opportunities for the widespread establishment of new, oil company-sponsored truck stops along newly-established routes, most featuring multiple-structure, standardized designs.

• Second Generation truck stops varied in physical size (many featuring multi-acre parking) and in the number of structures, and their type and placement within the lot. Some smaller stops were opened with most structures already constructed, and placed near the center of the facility, due to physical size constraints. Larger facilities occupied enough acreage that structures could be added at will, sometimes with seemingly random placement, but most often along the large frontal area of the property.

• Full-service restaurants began to replace the counter-and-stools lunch café of earlier years, at least at major oil company locations.

• Additional services began to be offered in the mid-late 1950s, but almost exclusively by oil company truck stops. The 1964 construction of the Iowa 80 truck stop would later set the standard for world-class truck stops with its inclusion of additional amenities. Among them: a barber shop, a dentistry facility, truck and trailer washing facilities, and a weigh scale.

• Most stops still built with no discernable or intended separation of truck and automobile traffic.

First and Second Generation truck stops were almost always situated close to or directly on the two-lane road that fed business to them, and parking was situated towards the rear of the lot. With the Interstate Highway System necessitating an exit from the highway, new Third Generation designs moved the

L. B. Heishman and his wife operated Heishman's Truck Stop on U.S. 11 at New Kingstown, Pennsylvania. A modern restaurant was added to an older service station to create this truck stop. It is seen here as it was in about 1960.

Near Yankton, South Dakota's junction of U.S. Highway 81 and State Route 50 (Nebraska Star Route), Kenneth Dreesen operated Kenny's Service (aka, "Kenny's Truck Arena," T-149). This appears to be a First Generation truck stop (possibly evidenced by the presence of a shingled roof farmhouse between the false front of the "Kenny's Service" building at left and the two-bay garage at center) that is striving towards Second Generation status. There exists extensive visual appeal: At left, the "Kenny's Truck Arena, Open 24 Hours, Motel" neon signage sits at roadside in front of the original false-front building, with a brick-construction café building behind and to the left of the signpole; three early 1950s-era globe-topped pumps sit on a concrete island; a red Coca-Cola chest cooler separates the fuel office from the service building; abundant homemade signage advertises, "Wash, Greasing," "Minnows," "We Buy Sell and Trade Guns," "Sporting Goods," "Live Bait," and "Ice." At right, a fourth pump (likely for diesel) sits under a stationlighter, while signage behind notes, "24 Hour Service," "Free Ice Water," "Minnows," "Diesel Fuels," and "Free Air." This location was no longer listed in Skelly's Truck Stop Directories by 1969.

main building towards center of the lot, with parking becoming available on the sides as well as in the back. The front of the building was still relegated to the fuel lanes.

THIRD GENERATION TRUCK STOPS

• Large oil company truck stops began to displace the Mom & Pop facilities and regional chains on a large scale. Their franchising-friendly programs fueled a growth-spurt that coincided with the continuing expansion of the Interstate Highway network.

• Random-placement of separate structures for separate services on the lot began to be replaced by a concept of increased effectiveness in the utilization of space with "all under one roof"-type constructions (the exception sometimes being the placement of an adjunct services/repair building away from major traffic lanes) and a pointed standardization of facility designs; PURE and Skelly oil companies pioneered this idea.

• The role of automotive traffic as a revenue source was re-examined; autos increasingly were separately accommodated on an expanding scale. At this point, truck and auto traffic were still allowed to freely intermix at entrances and exits. The transition from "truck stop" to "travel plaza" begins here, with the designated separation of automotive and truck services. Autos were almost always given preferential status by being directed towards the front of the facility, and truck traffic being shunted towards the sides or rear of the facility.

• Separation of traffic continued inside, with "truckers only" sections being established, and forcibly separated from tourist-traffic areas.

• Dormitory-style sleeping and showering facilities began to be replaced by individual motel-style rooms with showers, which appealed to motorists. As late as September 1969, a recently-opened Burns Bros. Truck Plaza south of Portland, Oregon, offered 10 doubles-style sleeping rooms. A "women-only" area included a bath. An additional four motel-type rooms were offered for husband and wife teams.

• Additional services often included such amenities as a truckers' store, a billiards room, and a barber shop.

As these Third Generation truck stops evolved, several constants emerged: While the truck stop exteriors became more industrial in appearance (with

PURE Truck Stop #528, located on Highway 192 at the junction with I-80 and I-29 in Council Bluffs, Iowa, dates from approximately 1965. Herb Honig operated this truck stop for at least a couple of years; by 1967, it was missing from the PURE Truck Stop Directory. Tymac's Restaurant can be seen at center, with "roomettes" immediately above. A late 1950s International Emeryville can be seen fueling at left; twin service bays are located at the back of the building, immediately to the right of the Emeryville.

In 1964, Hughes Millard's Skelly Truck Stop (T-202) was just a conceptual drawing, and the Sioux Oil Co. of Newcastle, Wyoming, was the proposed petroleum products supplier. By 1965 the finished truck stop was a reality on I-90, 1/2-mile west of the State Route 34 interchange, and included a fully-asphalted lot (gravel in this pre-opening photo notwithstanding). By 1967, Robert Nichols was the operator; Robert Towler was the Manager by 1968. Ken Montague had assumed the reins by 1969. When new owner Harold Riley took over in about 1973, he named Willie Ayala as manager. This unit had become a Getty Truck Stop by 1984.

the disappearance of the old farmhouse cafés and converted barns for truck service facilities), the interiors began to emphasize the domestic qualities of the earlier First and Second Generation truck stops, stressing "home made" meals, personalized service for both truck and driver, and amenities such as wood paneling on the walls, faux-wooden flooring, a brick faux fireplace, additional booths in the restaurant, carpeting in eating areas (replacing linoleum) and peripheral decoration that featured restored early-century visible-register gasoline pumps and period porcelain signage.

The "domesticity" that the Mom & Pop truck stops exhibited in their roadside offerings may have been roundly shunned by Big Oil's wholesale adoption of a more modern architectural style, but, ironically, the "domestic" *idea* was wholly accepted and advanced by the Big Oil truck stops, with the convention of adopting restaurant monikers such as, "Mom's Kitchen," "Grandma's Pantry," or the like.

Personalized service was extended both inside and out. Trucks could be dropped off at the fuel islands, and would be fueled by a friendly, uniformed attendant who would clean the windshields, check fluid levels, and thump the tires, before parking the rig in a handy spot, all while the driver consumed a "home-cooked" meal of meatloaf and mashed potatoes, just like mom used to make.

FOURTH GENERATION TRUCK STOPS

• With the near-completion of the Interstate Highway System by the mid-1980s, the demand for new truck stop constructions stabilized. In order to increase revenue streams with existing locations, oil companies began to expend additional efforts to attract non-truck traffic, specifically targeting the quick turnaround ("EZ Off, EZ On") aspects of their operations, as well as by segmenting some of their parking for larger recreational vehicles. These are typified by today's modern chain travel plazas: Flying J, T/A, Pilot, etc.

• In addition, truck stop sub-categories began to emerge:

-*Destination truck stops:* Large, all-encompassing truck stops featuring an array of eateries and available services; a "truck stop city" in effect. Iowa 80 in Walcott, Iowa, and Little America in Little America, Wyoming, typify the genre.

-*Transient truck stops:* Scaled-down versions of Destination truck stops, many of which are carry-over Third Generation stops; few new constructions of this type.

-*Pumpers:* Facilities designed and constructed to be simply fuel stops; basically just a "gas station" for trucks. Extraneous services such as expansive parking lots, mechanical services, sleeping facilities, and eateries are significantly minimized, or are completely eliminated. This creates cheaper and quicker transactions for truckers who are only interested in fueling; other services are postponed until a scheduled stop at a Destination truck stop.

• Each of the above truck stop sub-categories continues the practice of separating auto and truck traffic. Newer constructions (today's post-1980s "travel stops"), strive for segregation in both fueling and parking. Separate entrances and exits for trucks and cars facilitate this process. Inside however, all customers are allowed to intermix.

Additional sub-categories have been further identified. In her thesis, "A Home Away From Home: Telling The Story of the Trucking Industry Through the Preservation of 1960s Truck Stops," author Jessica Breitbach asserts that there are three main building types that demonstrate the progression of the truck stop industry from individually-owned ("Mom & Pop") stops to commercially-owned (Big Oil) stops. Those three types are: Converted Mom & Pop truck stops; Experimental truck stop prototypes; and Established truck stop prototypes. The Established truck stop prototypes are the direct result of the improvements and refinements of Experimental truck stop prototypes.

CONVERTED MOM & POP TRUCK STOPS

• Generally First Generation or early Second Generation truck stops that had often been converted from former farmhouses and barns.

• Adjoining buildings for additional services were added as conditions required, creating an ersatz truck stop "complex," with each building being constructed with a separate, individual purpose in mind, usually on a section of the property large enough to accommodate the structure, regardless of its location relative to the main roadside structure.

• Many of these Mom & Pop sites later joined established truck stop chains, which were almost entirely controlled by oil companies such as PURE.

• Some oil companies had established chains of truck stops as early as the mid-late 1950s. These were a simple networking of existing sites grouped beneath a single corporate umbrella.

• Sometimes corporate standards necessitated a modification of facilities before the site could be incorporated into the chain. In some instances, the modifications might be as simple as an addition of corporate logo signage; in others, a re-working of services offered and their associated building types might be called for.

It was this more complex revision of site structures, accompanied by the coming of the Interstate Highway System, that led oil companies to experiment with prototypes for new constructions.

EXPERIMENTAL TRUCK STOP PROTO-TYPES.

• The beginnings of the Third Generation truck stop.

• In the 1960s, oil companies provided the capital and the impetus to implement prototypical truck stop designs in an effort to begin the process of generating a cohesive appearance to the properties with which their brand and logo were associated.

• Popular modern architectural ideals were incorporated into the designs. Flat overhanging roofs, geo-

Southern 500 truck stops began in Charlotte, North Carolina, in the mid-1950s, becoming one of the first participants in the Esso-fleet brand program developed by Standard Oil Co. of New Jersey. Identical truck stops were built in Charlotte, Wilson, and Mount Airy, North Carolina, and in Society Hill, South Carolina, and they operated as Southern 500 into the 1970s. Today, only the Society Hill location operates as a truck stop (privately owned). Shown in this photo is the prototype building used for the operation, with all fuel islands arranged in a large lot behind the restaurant and store building. This photo dates from about 1960 and is believed to be the Wilson location.

metric forms, and large plate glass windows facing roadside predominated.

• Additional constructions were added on to the main structure instead of creating an entirely separate new building, as was the case with earlier First Generation and Second Generation truck stops.

ESTABLISHED TRUCK STOP PROTOTYPES

• Both Skelly and PURE implemented standardized designs that centered around the construction of one large building that housed many different services, such as restaurant, fueling services, restrooms, truck repair services, and sleeping accommodations. These standardized designs were the result of the refinement of many revisions of their Experimental truck stop prototypes.

• Skelly's and PURE's prototypes were the most visible and ubiquitous; they set a standard which was copied and modified for many other truck stop constructions. In practice, each company's early attempts at the standardization of truck stop architecture were strikingly similar: low-slung, rectangular-shaped concrete buildings; restaurants featuring roadside-facing massive plate glass windows located on one side of the building, with "RESTAURANT" neon signage above; main entrances to the buildings located at the center of the structure; oil company

SOHIO's first corporate truck stop opened in October of 1963, just outside of Ashland, Ohio. Christened Stop 250 for its location on Interstate 71 at U.S. 250, this site became a model for SOHIO truck stops throughout the 1960s. A large prefabricated building housed a store, a restaurant, and service facilities, with separate gas and diesel islands positioned along the road frontage side, all located in the middle of six acres of parking. This photo was taken during the opening week.

brand names prominently displayed in neon opposite from the RESTAURANT signage; graveled-dirt approaches leading to concrete fuel islands.

These truck stop designs were located at key interchanges all over the central and eastern portions of the U.S.: Skelly operated truck stops as far west as Colorado, and as far east as Mississippi; PURE operated truck stops from North Dakota to Florida. There is no known connection between Skelly's and PURE's truck stop architectural design divisions.

Efficiency was the key to good design and directly affected the internal and external layout of these Established Truck Stop Prototypes. A fueling counter (where a driver could pay for his fuel, or receive an itemized receipt of what was billed to his company), a truckers' store, a restaurant, a TV lounge, and sleeping and showering facilities were included. Dormitory-style sleeping and gang-shower facilities were replaced by individual sleeping rooms with showers, similar in design and intent to motel rooms. A gang shower room was sometimes included for truckers who wanted only a shower without renting a room for the night. Often, the shower was free if a certain amount of fuel had been pumped into the trucker's fuel tanks, or was available at a nominal charge.

Fuel Canopies became part of these Established Truck Stop Prototype designs in the late '60s. Until this point, fuel canopies were scarce at truck stops. The addition of canopies allowed for protection from the elements while trucks were being fueled and serviced, providing shade in the summer, and shielding from rain and snow in the winter.

NON-TRADITIONAL TRUCK STOP SUB-TYPOLOGIES

Additionally, certain specialty sub-types that defy the main categories outlined above can be identified:

TRAVEL STOP OPERATORS - *Stuckey's, Horne's, Nickerson Farms, etc.*

While not specifically categorized as truck stops, many of the early roadside establishments intended mostly for motorists also served as de facto truck stops. Early incarnations were located on highly-traveled rural two-lanes; later versions tended to be sited on rural Interstates. The most ubiquitous of the sub-types were Stuckey's, Hornes', and Nickerson Farms.

Stuckey's 28th location opened on U.S. 31-82 at Prattville, Alabama, in about 1953. It is shown here shortly after it opened.

Stuckey's locations were often sited at strategic highway points, such as where multiple highways converged. This unit, #21, at South Pittsburg, Tennessee, was no exception. When opened in 1951, it was located on U.S. 41, a major north-south route, as well as U.S. 64-72, a major east-west route.

The earliest of this sub-type began to be seen on America's highways in the late '30s, and typically consisted of a small, rectangular-shaped lot sited on a rural two-lane. They sported limited parking, most of which was designated for auto traffic. Graveled approaches and exits were the norm, as was the offering of two to four fuel pumps, with usually not more than one pump (if that many) dispensing diesel fuel. A small gift-type shop featuring restrooms, and a luncheon counter offering a narrow selection of food choices, served to round out the list of available services; later incarnations traded a hamburgers-and-hot-dogs counter for a more formal sit-down restaurant. Due to the few-and-far-between nature of early truck stops, some of these tourist-focused facilities effectively became truck stops due to their convenient locations along well-traveled truck routes, especially in the 1940s and '50s when gasoline-engine trucks and two-lane highways still predominated.

The *Stuckey's Corporation* can legitimately be considered as the progenitor of this Tourist Gas Station sub-type. In 1937, William S. Stuckey and his wife Ethel opened a small roadside stand in Eastman, Georgia, and sold pecans and pecan-based candies to passing motorists.

The idea was so successful that two more roadside stands were built. A fourth stand was operating, this one in Hilliard, Florida, by 1941. The chain continued to expand after the WWII, and was bolstered by the building of the Interstate Highway System in the '60s. Approximately 375 *Stuckey's Pecan Shoppes* were eventually in operation, most sited at Interstate Highway exits, with their by-then signature distinctive roof design and pastel-turquoise roof tiles fully visible to passing traffic from the freeway. Candies, hot dogs, novelties, clean restrooms, and an extended association with the nation-wide TEXACO gasoline brand helped to expand the Stuckey's brand's livelihood (although some locations sold Aetna, Sinclair, Pan-Am, Phillips 66, DX, or Shell gasolines, especially in the early years). A failed 1960s effort aimed at providing motel-type lodging resulted in only two locations offering motel facilities.

After a couple of ownership changes, the teal-roofed Stuckey's brand continues today, albeit in a highly metamorphosed form as a gas station/Convenience Store clone sporting royal blue roofs, or teamed as a tag-along to certain Dairy Queen outlets. Virtually all are Interstate accessible.

Horne's, a small chain of Florida-based nut-and-candy stores with a similar format to that of Stuckey's, ostensibly began as a rebuttal by a disgruntled former Stuckey's employee. Bob Horne, a Stuckey's candy salesman, opened his initial Horne's location on U.S. 1, near Bayard, Florida, south of Jacksonville in the early 1950s. Following Stuckey's lead, Horne's maintained a close association with TEXACO (but also operated sites featuring Shell, Standard Oil and GULF gasolines), with each location sporting a signature roof design and color; in this instance, yellow roof tiles.

Unlike Stuckey's, Horne's often provided sit-down restaurants, and motel lodging at several sites, with the lodging locations often offering guests a swimming pool. The Horne's chain never achieved the gaudy location numbers flashed by Stuckey's, but was nevertheless quite successful. As near as can be determined, only a few locations remain extant, all plucky, locally-owned remnants located somewhere between Virginia and Florida that have survived despite the collapse of the corporate owned chain.

Nickerson Farms operated 70 gasoline/restaurant locations in 17 states, at their peak. Similar to Horne's, Nickerson Farms had its beginnings with a disgruntled Stuckey's employee; in this case, Mr. I. J. Nickerson, and in this case, in the late 1950s. I. J. Nickerson had been responsible for the franchising of the first Stuckey's west of the Mississippi River in 1957, which he located in Eldon, Missouri. Differences between Nickerson and William Stuckey led to Nickerson rebranding his store to his newly-created *Nickerson Farms* brand. Like Hornes' but unlike Stuckey's, Nickerson insisted on a full-service sit-down restaurant for his locations. Also unlike Stuckey's, Nickerson standardized all Nickerson Farms locations, in 1966, to one fuel supplier: Kansas City's Skelly Oil Co. By 1967, the program was gaining ground, with 21 Nickerson Farms/Skelly combinations in operation in eight midwestern states.

All Nickerson Farms outlets subsequent to the initial Eldon, Missouri, site featured eight pumps under a canopy placed in front of the entrance, with each site featuring the Nickerson Farms signature red-tiled roofline topping pseudo-English Tudor style architecture. All locations were sited at Interstate Highway access points. Unlike Stuckey's, which allowed franchising (and gave Nickerson the right to rebrand his original store), *Nickerson Farms* remained 100% company-owned. The company changed hands several times until finally ceasing to exist in about 1980.

Internet websites report that additional, albeit smaller but similar chains of the Tourist Gas Station sub-type, such as B. Lloyd's, Atkinson's, and Saxon's, were also operating in the South from the mid-1930s onward.

TURNPIKE STATIONS

Turnpikes are defined as an expressway from which tolls are collected from the user. They are common in the eastern U.S., and can be found as far

The Will Rogers Turnpike in Oklahoma opened in 1957. One of the most unique features of the roadway was this lane-straddling plaza located outside of Vinita, Oklahoma. During the 1950s and 1960s, the plaza featured The Glass House Restaurant and CONOCO branded truck and tourist stop facilities, but today houses one of the largest McDonald's in the U.S. This photo dates from about 1959.

In the early 1950s, extensions were added to the original mileage of the Pennsylvania Turnpike. GULF bid on and received the franchise for the travel plaza operations on these new sections of the highway. In some instances, temporary facilities were constructed, housing the offices for the GULF turnpike station and a small Howard Johnson's snack bar. Most of these temporary facilities were replaced by full plazas within a few years. This photo dates from 1952.

west as Oklahoma. Fueling and restaurant facilities, as well as truck stops, have often been included in the design and layout of turnpikes, helping to negate the need for travelers to exit the turnpike in search of services. The PURE Oil Co. operated at least a couple of turnpike station truck stops in the middle and late 1960s. For example, the Knute Rockne Service Plaza, and the Wilbur Shaw Service Plaza were a set of nearly identical turnpike stations located near Rolling Prairie, Indiana, on I-80/90 (Indiana Toll Rd). The Towpath Service Plaza, and the Great Lakes Service Plaza, located in Ohio on I-80/90 (Ohio Turnpike) west of Cleveland, Ohio, is another example; in each instance, a truck stop was located on opposite sides of the highway, one each for both eastbound and westbound traffic.

In Chicago, Illinois, the Tri-State Tollway offers an alternative version of PURE's design. The *Oasis* chain sited service facilities to span the northbound and southbound lanes, and places restaurants, gift shops, and rest rooms in a glass-encased building that overlooks all highway lanes and provides diners with a breathtaking view of traffic passing beneath them. Fueling facilities are sited alongside the highway, at the exits. Originally, five Oasis locations were financed and constructed by the Standard Oil Company of Indiana in 1959. Currently, seven Oasis locations are in operation, all featuring Mobil fuels and a varied array of fast foods.

Besides the Oasis chain in Illinois, one of the more

Where right of way acquisition on the Pennsylvania Turnpike permitted, full service plazas were developed. Facilities such as this one served as a complete GULF fuel facility and a full service Howard Johnson restaurant. This photo shows one such facility in 1959.

The Will Rogers Turnpike in Oklahoma opened in 1957 and at one of the service plazas, Phillips 66 and Howard Johnson's held the operator concessions. Elaborate multi-pump service station facilities were typical of these high-volume service plaza stations, which also served as truck stops along the toll roads. This photo dates from 1958.

famous of the freeway-spanning turnpike stations is the *Glass House*, located on I-44 (Will Rogers Turnpike) near Vinita, Oklahoma. The Glass House mimicked the Oasis designs, placing eateries, gift shops, and rest rooms in a glass-encased building spanning four lanes of traffic and a median, but placed the fueling at each turnpike exit point, on opposite sides of the freeway. Originally sporting a sit-down restaurant, the McDonald's hamburger chain currently operates the eatery in this facility, which at 23,135 square feet, was once the largest McDonald's in the world, with seating for more than 300 customers.

A notable mention is *The Great Platte River Road Archway Monument* that spans I-80 near Kearney, Nebraska. It is similar in design and intent to the above-mentioned traveler-oriented, turnpike-spanning highway stops, featuring food, fuel, and souvenirs, but overlooks a freeway instead of a turnpike.

ON TODAY'S HIGHWAYS

A trend towards consolidation began in the late 1960s, both in the oil industry in general, and in the truck stop industry more specifically. Many stalwart oil companies from decades earlier began to be swallowed up by larger or competing concerns. Union 76 began to absorb the PURE Oil Co. and its approximately 300 truck stops in the mid-1960s. Getty Oil Co. began assimilating the Skelly Oil Co. and all of its nearly 220 associated truck stops in the early 1980s. (Getty in turn, was later swallowed by TEXACO, which was later assimilated by Shell, and then spun off to Chevron). Other smaller, regional chains began to be absorbed by larger corporations during this time also: Husky Oil Co's. U.S. truck stops were sold off to Flying J; Shamrock's 26 truck stops were purchased by Ultramar, which later became Ultramar Diamond Shamrock; Blue & White Service's 11 truck stops in Indiana simply ceased to exist due to uncertain economic times and questionable management practices.

Today, First and Second Generation truck stops, in their original forms or anything closely resembling such, are essentially non-existent. Third Generation truck stops are difficult to unearth, but a few can still be located with diligence; most are likely to have suffered significant re-structuring that is likely to have assumed some of the more ubiquitous characteristics of today's travel plazas.

Travel plazas are by far the most abundant extant

Nighttime at a truckstop is always a good time for a meal, and respite for the night. In the few photos of modern truck stops included in this book, as many night shots as possible have been used, as these shots best capture the essence of today's facilities. The fuel islands at this Flying J outlet located at Kenly, North Carolina, are just settling in for the night in this 2009 photo. *Jason Henderson photo*

With the purchase of Flying J, Pilot has sold off some locations that duplicate facilities or no longer fit within their marketing plans. This outlet is located between Dunn and Benson, North Carolina, and was photographed in the process of transition to Love's in early 2011. *Jason Henderson photo*

Dedicated transports are set up on continuous runs to keep truck stops supplied with fuels. At Toms Brook, Virginia, a Love's fleet transport drops fuel to refill underground tanks. The night shift busily continues to serve all travelers' needs. *Jason Henderson photo*

In 2003, Pilot purchased the travel center operations of the Williams Companies. This location, at Florence, South Carolina, rebranded from Williams to Pilot at that time, and is seen here in a 2009 photo.

Pilot Travel Centers today include spacious lots, separate auto and truck entrances and fueling positions, branded fast food, and complete truckers and convenience stores. This Pilot Travel Center is located on Interstate 64 at Grayson, Kentucky and was photographed in 2010.

truck stop archetype, followed by remnant Fourth Generation truck stops. The bulk of the travel plazas are more often operated by truck stop operating corporations such as TravelCenters of America (T/A), Pilot, Flying J, Love's, Williams, and Giant, as opposed to earlier practices, in which truck stops were operated by oil companies and offered only that oil company's brand of fuels. Each of these travel plaza operators offer major-brand fuels at all of their locations, but are not necessarily directly owned by any major oil company. For example, in recent years, TravelCenters of America listed in excess of 160 travel plazas operating in more than 40 states, featuring fuels branded by nearly 20 different oil companies: 76, AMOCO, ARCO, BP, Chevron, CITGO, CONOCO, EXXON, Marathon, Mobil, Phillips 66, Shell, SUNOCO, T/A, Tesoro, TEXACO, Ultramar, and Valero.

Similarly, more recent offerings at T/A locations have included fast food brands including A&W, Arby's, Baskin Robbins, Blimpie, Burger King, Chester Fried Chicken, Church's Fried Chicken, Cinnabon, Cold Stone Creamery, Dairy Queen, Domino's Pizza, Dunkin' Donuts, Highway Café, Hot Stuff Pizza, Hunt Brothers Pizza, Kentucky Fried Chicken, Krispy Kreme Donuts, Long John Silver's, McDonald's, Mrs. B's Pastry, Noble Roman's Pizza Express, Pizza Hut, Popeye's, Quizno's, Sbarro Pizza, Seattle's Best, Starbucks, Subway, Taco Bell, Taco Time, TCBY, Tim Horton's, and Wendy's.

Changes in the corporations that operate truck stops and travel plazas have been supplemented by evolutionary changes in the trucks themselves that these facilities have been built to service. Most notable for the truck stop and travel plaza operators are technological advances in engine design and aerodynamics that allow fully-loaded, 80,000-pound trucks to achieve 7 to 8 mpg at freeway speeds, which is nearly double the 4 to 5 mpg that slower, lower-horsepower trucks were achieving in the '60s. The negative effect this innovation has had on fuel sales for these corporations is partially offset by the greater number of trucks operating on U.S. highways.

Today's trucks typically sport sleeper "condos" that often include all of the amenities of home, or the typical motel room: Microwave oven, twin double beds, a refrigerator, a shower, a closet, satellite TV, a small desk, air conditioning, and a dining table. These conveniences are handy for the trucker, but siphon business from the truck stop operator in the form of decreased motel room demand, decreased restaurant sales, and decreased shower sales. (In 1966, an overnight room at a typical Skelly Truck Stop was $3.50, and a typical truck tractor cost $20,000; In the late 2000s, an overnight room can cost $60.00 or more, and a truck tractor well in excess of $150,000.) Truck stops and travel plazas are responding by charging a parking fee for stays extending beyond a specified number of hours.

Marathon reintroduced the Speedway brand for company-operated pumper stations in the mid-1970s. After several chains were purchased that included truck stop operations, the Speedway name was applied to what was, at the time, the largest oil company-owned and operated truck stop network. In a market repositioning maneuver in 2001, all of the Speedway truck stop locations, such as this one in Corbin, Kentucky, were sold to Pilot and rebranded during 2002.

When truckers shut down their rigs at truck stops for extended downtime periods for sleep, or other off-duty activities, they typically will allow their truck's engine to idle to provide electrical power for lighting, air conditioning, and other services in the sleeper. Today's 475- to 600-horsepower diesel engines will typically burn a gallon of diesel fuel per hour at idle, spewing unnecessary hydrocarbons into the atmosphere. A growing trend at many truck stops and travel plazas is the installation of "shore power;" i.e., parking lot hookups that allow the trucker to (for a price) hook up his rig to electrical power, cable TV, Wi-Fi Internet, and air conditioning. Because no "all-night idling" is allowed at locations where this service is available, truckers are obligated to comply and purchase the shore hookup, or find another travel plaza in which to spend downtime. On-board electrical generator units powered by a small gasoline- or propane-powered engine that negate the need to allow the main diesel to idle all night are gaining in popularity.

Wilco's first full-service truck stop was this facility, which opened in 1990 on Interstate 81 in Raphine, Virginia. Wilco was one of the first travel center operators to incorporate nationally-branded fast food facilities into its outlets, a practice that is almost universal today. It is seen here in 2009. *Jason Henderson photo*

In 1934 Roy Cline opened a small service station at a rural location in central New Mexico. Within three years the location had been bypassed by the routing of the then-new U.S. 66. Roy relocated his service station to the new location along U.S. 66 and continued to add to the facility for many years. At the time this photo was taken in the early 1970s, the facility was serving as a truck stop selling both Chevron and Shell fuels, and featured a restaurant and large retail travel store. Since then, the facility was again enlarged, and is still in operation today.

Chapter 2
ONE-STOPS, LITTLE AMERICA, AND IOWA 80

Before there were today's travel plazas, there were the 1940s, '50s and '60s truck stops. And before there were truck stops, there were… Travel plazas…?

Cross-country auto travel began in the early 1900s. Two attempts to travel cross-country by auto had failed miserably, but in 1903, a Vermont doctor named Horatio Nelson Jackson was ostensibly the first person to complete the treacherous coast-to-coast run by automobile.

Jackson departed San Francisco on May 23, 1903 in a 20-horsepower Winton automobile, and arrived at his destination in New York two months and 5,600 miles later. There were no gas stations (gas was purchased by the bucketful at general stores), no road maps, and no highway signage along his route; in fact, there were no "highways" at all. Just simple, rutted, muddy, farm-to-market roads suited only for usage by livestock-drawn wagons. There were a scant 150 miles of paved "highways" in the U.S. at that time, and most were located in large eastern cities.

There is no known tally of how many of those paved miles Jackson might have traveled. However, from about Green River, Wyoming, eastward to near Fort Wayne, Indiana, he toured a route that would roughly approximate that of the future Lincoln Highway, the beginnings of which were still more than a decade away.

ONE-STOPS

In 1916, the concept for The Lincoln Highway, the proposed "coast-to-coast rock highway," was in its infancy, but was on its way to becoming a major east-west construction. After its inception, during the late 1920s and early '30s, the first of a unique roadside business archetype was beginning to spring up along its edges, and simultaneously, along the edges of some of the other emerging named highways of the era. At the time, they were called "One-Stops" because they offered the automobile traveler virtually everything needed for the continuance of

The Diamonds was a famous roadside restaurant and truck stop on U.S. 66 at Villa Ridge, Missouri. The original Diamonds, simply a restaurant at that time, was opened in 1927 by Spencer Groff. After a devastating fire in 1948, the facility was rebuilt on the original site, shown in the older photo here, and was known until recently as the Tri State Truck Stop. The Diamonds relocated in 1967 to the site shown in the later photo for easier access to the newly constructed Interstate 44. The rooftop sign from the original site was brought to the new location. Multiple gasoline brands were sold here, and a full motel was part of the offering. Sadly, all that remains today is the motel, as the Diamonds is no more.

The Dixie Truckers Home has a legitimate claim to being the first independent truck stop in America. Founded as a service station and diner in 1928 by John and Viola Geske and Viola's father, J. P. Walters, the concept of a truck stop did not exist when the Dixie Truckers Home was constructed. By the middle 1930s, they began marketing themselves as a truck stop, and bunkrooms and cabins were added. Located along the famous U.S. 66 in McLean, Illinois, the Dixie Truckers Home was ideally positioned for growth. John and Viola's daughter, C.J. and her husband Chuck Beeler, became involved in the business in the 1950s and saw it through a devastating fire in 1965 along with the rebuilding of the operation into a modern truck stop. The Beeler's retired in 2003, selling the operation to an independent operator who modernized the facility. It operates today as the Dixie Travel Plaza. The earlier photo here shows the Dixie Truckers Home about 1950, then later after the rebuild following the 1965 fire.

HALFWAY HOUSE, RESTAURANT AND SERVICE STATION, U.S. 25, WILLIAMSTOWN, KY.

U.S. Highway 25 was a major north-south truck route during much of the 20th century, and truck stops were found all along its length. One of the best known was the Halfway House Truck Stop, at Williamstown, Kentucky. The operation started in the 1930s as many other First Generation trucks stops did: simply a restaurant and service station. Over the years, the restaurant was expanded and a motel was added for truckers and tourists. Standard Oil of Kentucky products were sold here throughout its existence. The oldest photo dates from around 1940. The second photo shows that company drivers, in this case those specifically working for A&P, had discovered the restaurant and began to make it a regular stop. The latest photos show it in its sunset, after Interstate 75 had bypassed it in the 1960s and truckers no longer felt it necessary to make the detour for a stop.

automotive travel in "one stop"—fuel, food, lodging, and occasionally, additional amenities. For all intents and purposes, these were early "travel plazas" in the respect that no preference was given to either auto or truck traffic, as there was little or no cross-country trucking at this time.

By the mid-late 1950s, Third Generation truck stops, still mostly operated by Mom & Pop, but whose territory was being increasingly encroached upon by oil companies' new truck stop constructions, had effectively segregated their purchasing traffic to favor truckers, and had relegated auto trade to a secondary status. Oil company truck stops located at "E-Z Off, E-Z On" interchanges along the Interstates re-examined this dictum in the 1960s, and began to favor auto travelers (of whom there were many more) with the logic that auto travelers often supported their de-

cision to stop for services at one location over another with the argument that if the establishment was popular with truckers, the restaurant must be good; "Truckers know all of the best places to eat" on any given highway. This was, effectively, the "re-birth" of the "One-Stop," though now re-named "travel plaza."

Although not as slick and glitzy as their current "travel plaza" incarnations along today's sleek four-lane Interstates, the 1920s and '30s-era one-stops were as comfortable and down-homey as the slower-paced two-lanes on which they resided. Likely, there would be a house-with-canopy type of gas station with perhaps as many as four fuel pumps. The pump island would be accessible to cars under the canopy, while the side with no canopy could accommodate tractor-trailer trucks, almost all of which were still gasoline powered, as diesel power had not yet been adopted as the standard for cross-country trucks. Some one-stops were built with the gas station building separate from the fueling islands, and these islands most often offered no canopies. Just as likely, in either configuration, there would be a small café or lunch room, and, in some cases, perhaps a half-dozen or so cabins for overnighting.

In an article entitled, "'One-Stops' on The Lincoln Highway," published in the Fall, 1997 issue of *The Lincoln Highway Forum* magazine, author Lyell Henry profiles several of the most famous of The Lincoln Highway one-stops, including Niland's Corner, located in Colo, Iowa; King Tower, located in Tama, Iowa; and Twin Towers, located in Cedar Rapids, Iowa. The inception of these "pre-travel plaza" travel plazas are detailed below.

Colo Cabin Camp, located at Niland's Corner in Colo, Iowa, circa early 1940s.

NILAND'S CORNER; COLO, IOWA

A classic "Mom & Pop"-operated one-stop, Niland's Corner had its origins when Charlie Reed saw a potential business opportunity laid at the doorstep of his Lincoln Highway farmhouse in 1923 with a re-routing of the Jefferson Highway. Located at the "corner" of The Lincoln Highway's intersection with the Jefferson Highway (which ran from Winnipeg, Manitoba, to New Orleans, Louisiana), Reed opened the L & J Standard filling station. Brisk business provided expansions in 1926 and 1930, including an enlarged version of the original station, the addition of a small food stand (later enlarged to become a café), and the beginnings of what would eventually become a 12-unit cabin camp. In the 1930s, the complex began 24-hour a day operation. Reed worked the station, while nephews from the Niland side of his family ran the café and motel. In the early '50s, café hours were trimmed and there were no meals available between the hours of 1:00am and 6:00am. Charlie Reed retained sole proprietorship of the gas station until his death in 1966. The café and cabin camp continued to be run by the Nilands.

Following WWII the Colo Cabin Camp became the Colo Motel when an expansion increased lodging offerings to 18 units, each sporting heat, air conditioning, and private baths.

The 1960s brought considerable change to Niland's Corner. In 1962, The Lincoln Highway (now U.S. Highway 30) was realigned to a route about a mile south of its former alignment. In 1966, the completion of Interstate 80 pushed traffic even further south, and the businesses at Niland's Corner began to slump from a downturn in trade. At this point, Reed began closing the gas station for a few hours overnight and gave up 24-hour operations. Charlie Reed passed on in 1966, and the gas station was closed permanently less than a year later.

The Colo Motel was partially remodeled to provide rental apartments, and only five motel units remained for overnight rental. The café heavily cut its hours to a 6:30am-to-8:00pm schedule (weekdays only), then closed permanently in 1991. In 1995, the Niland's ceased renting out the converted apartments, bringing to a close a three-generation, 68-year run for one of the first pre-truck stops in the U.S. The café building, the gas station building, and part of the motel complex, as well as the Colo Motel neon roadside signage, currently remain extant.

KING TOWER; TAMA, IOWA

Originally from Nebraska, Wesley W. Mansfield relocated to Belle Plaine, Iowa, in 1925. His involvement with the management of several Belle Plaine movie theaters provided him with a solid-base business acumen, which, in 1931, he used as a springboard to launch his vision of a prosperous roadside establishment: "The King One-Stop Service Station."

This early incarnation of his "One-Stop" vision centered on the "Service Station" aspect of the name, providing only auto-related services, while lacking any available meals or lodging. The site prospered as a favorite of cross-country truckers due to its prime location along The Lincoln Highway. Several years

King Tower Café in Tama, Iowa, circa late 1950s.

later, when a re-routing of The Lincoln Highway bypassed Belle Plaine, Mansfield chose a 15-acre site upon which to relocate. The new construction was named "The King Tower" and was heralded as "central Iowa's most modern one-stop service." It consisted of a café, a garage, and a CONOCO gas station. By 1939, Mansfield's King Tower one-stop also offered an 18-unit cabin complex for motorists, each sporting full bathroom facilities. Mansfield nodded to The Lincoln's cross-country trucker traffic by including 24-hour wrecker service and a two-story showers/dormitory/fuel island building flanking twin fuel pump islands. The King "Tower" part of the name was exemplified by the 20-foot tower that extended above the building's second floor. On the east- and west-facing sides of the Tower was the word, "GAS," spelled out vertically in blinking red neon. Purportedly, these blinking letters were visible for more than a half-mile in either direction along the two-lane Lincoln Highway.

The King Tower complex thrived during WWII and the following postwar period, operating 24 hours a day, seven days a week, with a café that eventually was expanded to accommodate 140 people. A souvenir/gift store offering "Indian" curios was added in the early 1950s, likely much to the delight of East Coast motorists who were yearning to experience the "real West." An expansive neon SOUVENIRS sign, featuring a beautifully-crafted neon Indian in full headdress regalia, alerted motorists to the upcoming opportunity to purchase gifts for the folks back home.

But, by 1965, times were changing. Mansfield and his wife retired and deeded the King Tower complex

to J. Leonard Taylor, a Tower employee since 1949. All seemed well—for now. However, less than a year later, I-80 opened across Iowa. Traffic on The Lincoln Highway plummeted. Sales at the King Tower followed the curve. The gas station was the first casualty, closing in the late '60s; the two-story truckers' showers/dormitory/fuel island building was razed in about 1970. Rental of the cabins ceased shortly thereafter.

Today, the King Tower, one of The Lincoln Highway's pre-eminent one-stop, pre-truck stop, pre-travel plazas, exists in an arrested state of decay, and serves today's Lincoln Highway travelers mostly as a rehabilitated look into pre-Interstate life on the highway.

THE TWIN TOWERS; CEDAR RAPIDS, IOWA

Unlike Tama's King Tower, Cedar Rapids' Twin Towers one-stop sported *two* towers atop the largest building along their Lincoln Highway roadside frontage. And like the towers it features, there were actually twin incarnations of The Twin Towers, the first one pre-dating Tama's King Tower by a year or so.

In 1930, Johnny Cox was operating a 20-cabin lodging establishment, headquartered in an old log cabin, known appropriately as "The Log Cabin Tourist Camp." The Log Cabin Tourist Camp was sited on 27 acres east of Cedar Rapids, on The Lincoln Highway.

By 1931, the business had expanded to provide two 24-hour gas stations, a grocery, and a café. Additional expansion a short while later provided an opportunity to rebuild the café, add the twin roadside-facing towers, and expand one of the gas station buildings to provide a second floor truckers' shower

The Twin Towers in Cedar Rapids, Iowa, circa 1939.

facility and dormitory, making this one-stop a de facto early truck stop.

Towards the end of the 1930s, Cox learned of plans to re-route a portion of The Lincoln Highway away from his establishment. He quickly purchased a 30-acre plot along the new road alignment, and, in 1939, opened a new one-stop complex with twin towers on the façade of the café (although of a different design than the towers at the Log Cabin). He named the new complex "The Twin Towers." The new Twin Towers also featured a 24-hour service station, and five duplex cabins.

Cox sold the Twin Towers to an unidentified owner, who re-sold it in 1941 to "Dutch" and Evelyn Winegar, who operated it until 1959. During their ownership, the Winegars added 11 cabins, and re-modeled the café twice, bringing the total customer capacity to 155 persons, including the patrons of a newly-added soda fountain. Additionally, a party room and dance floor were fashioned in the base-ment. Leakage of the twin towers forced their re-moval during one of the remodelings, leaving it The Twin Towers in name only.

In 1959, a land development company purchased The Twin Towers from the Winegars, and continued to operate the complex until they razed it in 1963 to build a supermarket; no trace of the Twin Tow-ers was allowed to remain. However, the original (Log Cabin) Twin Towers still exists in a modified form as a twin-towered apartment building. The old Log Cabin office building, a shower building, and one remaining tourist cabin have been converted to housing units, with all of their original identifying features obliterated by the remodeling process.

All of the above operations, and many similar ones springing up around the U.S. during this pe-riod, were the direct result of many 1920s munici-palities' practice of providing free campgrounds for auto tourists. These free campgrounds were designed to entice the tourists to spend some dollars purchas-ing supplies in their towns. When many free camps began to charge fees later in the decade, private auto camps began to appear, many featuring cabins, gas stations, cafés, and grocery stores; essentially, the birth of the "one-stop."

LITTLE AMERICA, WYOMING

The establishment that came to be the largest one-stop on The Lincoln Highway, and later the largest truck stop in the U.S., was Covey's Little America, located east of Granger, Wyoming, near the junction of The Lincoln Highway (Highway 30) and Highway 30 North.

Covey's Little America began as a one-stop on The Lincoln Highway in 1936 as a product of the organi-zation of the Covey Gas and Oil Co. by S. M. Covey. (The current Flying J travel plaza chain has direct lineage to this early fuel supplier). Via a multi-decade metamorphosis, including a relocation to what later became I-80, Little America became a combination one-stop/truck stop; later "the world's largest gas sta-tion"/truck stop; and was the precursor to the Iowa 80 truck stop, located near Walcott, Iowa, which cur-rently claims the "World's Largest Truck Stop" title.

A late-1940s or early-1950s shot of Covey's Little America, facing north-west. Signage and lodging at left, main restaurant/cocktail lounge/gift shop building at center, and Mobile branded gas station at right.

This westward-looking early 1960s shot of Covey's Little America was taken on a busy day. Gasoline pumps are now of early 1960s design and the pump islands feature efficient fluorescent lighting; gone are the 1940s-era pumps with stationlighters. Rooftop signage indicates that Mr. Covey has now converted this travelers' stop from his former Mobile brand to the Sinclair brand.

The extensive list of amenities that Little America offered in its early one-stop years anticipated the variety of services that later travel plazas would embrace. Ostensibly, Little America was birthed sporting a two-pump gas station, 12 "cabins," and a 23-seat café. By about decade later, Little America's gas station offered eight pumps. A cocktail lounge/dance floor, known as "The Palm Room" (sporting faux palm trees, a south seas island theme, a piano, and a dance floor) had been added; the café had expanded to become a full-fledged restaurant ("Coffee Shop"); the "cabins" had been converted to a "Lodge" and a "Hotel" offered a few rooms located above The Palm Room. Additionally, there were expanded restrooms for customers. The addition of an ice cream and soda fountain helped travelers wash away The Lincoln Highway's road dust. The Little America complex became so large, that, until a devastating fire in about 1949 that forced its relocation, it spanned both the north and south sides of The Lincoln Highway.

When rebuilt after the fire, Little America was relocated to follow a realignment of the Lincoln Highway. At this point, S. M. Covey, Little America's originator, began to publicly acknowledge the impetus for the moniker of his enterprise. As a child sheepherder in the 1890s, he'd laid over on the western Wyoming plains during a night of a frightful, sub-zero blizzard, nearly freezing to death. Many years later, after viewing images of Admiral Richard Byrd's establishment of the "Little America" base in the Antarctic in 1928, Covey was reminded of his near-death experience that night. He vowed to return to the spot of that occurrence, and establish a haven of refuge for those traveling this desolate section of desert. Naturally, Covey chose the name, "Little America" as an acknowledgment to Admiral Byrd's crew, whom had similarly suffered in extreme conditions.

Covey's newly-rebuilt Little America sported a "great sign" that emulated a shape that approximated an abstracted, elongated, continental outline of Antarctica. At this point, Covey also adopted the image of a penguin to serve as mascot and trademark. A penguin, later named "Emperor," was shipped from Antarctica, but died before arrival in Wyoming. Emperor's stuffed remains are on display in the Little America main building, along with a commemorative plaque detailing the penguin's trip from Antarctica, and its untimely death in transit to port in Boston.

By the mid-1950s, Little America's earlier eight-pump gas station had transformed itself into "The World's Largest Gas Station." The majority of those pumps pumped diesel, and thus by default, made Little America not only "The World's Largest Gas Station," but also, "The World's Largest Truck Stop," although its "World's Largest Truck Stop" claim wasn't heavily heralded.

The original Little America's gas station was branded "Covey Gas & Oil Co." By the time of, or slightly before, the 1949 fire, Covey Gas & Oil Co. began to display its "Mobile" brand (not to be confused with Socony-Vacuum Oil Company's and later Mobil Oil Company's Mobil brand) for its gas station operations at Little America.

The re-build of Little America saw the original two-pump gas station replaced by one sporting 20 pumps (later expanded to 55); the original 12 "cabins" had become 110 motel rooms (later expanded to 160); the cocktail lounge (minus the dance floor) had been greatly expanded ("Try our famous Buffalo Cocktail!"); and by the 1950s, the original 23-seat café had been re-built to accommodate 300 hungry patrons, in both a coffee shop (160 person capacity) and a formal dining room restaurant.

A 1951 brochure describes "Little America's Truck Terminal" thus: "Year-round, 24-hour Truck Service. One-Stop for Diesel Fuel, Truck Pit, Truck Rates, Garage… Wholesale, Retail… Trucker's Free Shower, Fast Coffee Service!"

For the auto traveler, one-stop attributes of this self-proclaimed "Queen of The Highways" were similarly spotlighted: "America's largest one-stop travel center!" – "Mmmm… Smell that coffee, taste that steak!" – "One stop for gas, oil… complete service! Free ice water too!" – "Giant, soft Mello Freeze cones" – "Luxurious free lounges… comfortable chairs… soft carpets."

Easterners traveling The Lincoln by auto were particularly targeted in this brochure: "Revel in your first visit to our souvenir and gift shop, where you'll find mementos for remembrance of your trip through the romantic West. Beautiful leather goods, gorgeous carved woods, authentic Indian jewelry of beaten silver and turquoise… exquisite copper knick knacks… Western gift dishes depicting scenes of the golden past. Gifts you and your friends will treasure. Ideal for parties, birthdays, anniversaries… or for fun! Mailed anywhere."

Little America's corporate name was changed from Covey Petroleum Corp. to Little America Refining Co. (LARCO) in the early 1950s. Shortly thereafter, in 1952, S. M. Covey turned over daily operations of all Little America properties to son-in-law Earl Holding and his wife Carol. By now Little America had become an enormous empire that included a gigantic

motor lodge in downtown Salt Lake City: "Covey's New America Motor Lodge and Coffee Shop," which included 225 air-conditioned rooms with radios and telephones and a Marriott's "Hot Shoppes" drive-in restaurant. Other motor lodges were located in Idaho Falls, Pocatello, and Twin Falls, Idaho. Covey's Mobile branded gas stations included "Johnson's Super Service" in Laketown, Utah; "Baugh's Service Station" in Logan, Utah; and "Covey's Mobile Service" in Border, Wyoming.

The Sinclair Oil & Refining Co. purchased Covey's LARCO corporation in 1955, and Little America began displaying the Sinclair brand. In 1959, seven years after Earl Holding assumed control of the Little America properties, S. M. Covey passed on.

In 1965, Earl Holding expanded the Little America operations by opening a second Little America branded location. Sited on the western outskirts of Cheyenne, Wyoming, the operation sported 50 pumps, and a respectable catalog of trucker-oriented services. However, a 9-hole golf course, formal dining facilities, swimming pools, and emphasis on first-class tourist accommodations tend to characterize this location as more of a resort than a truck stop.

In 1967, Earl Holding purchased a mothballed Mobil Oil Co. refinery in Casper, Wyoming, to supply the original Little America travelers' stop, and his newly-opened resorts located in Cheyenne, and Salt Lake City, with petroleum products. A growing distribution network allowed for wholesale supply of petroleum products into the Colorado, Idaho, western South Dakota, and Utah markets.

By the late 1960s, a growth spurt at the original Little America required as many as 240 people to be under employment, approximately 50 of whom lived on premises. A Little America-operated bus line transported a majority of the remainder of the employees to and from their jobs from the towns of Green River, Rock Springs, Lyman, and Mountain View. A fire truck, hydrants, extinguishers, and employees comprised Little America's volunteer fire department.

The Atlantic-Richfield Oil Co. (ARCO) merged with Sinclair in the late 1960s. Government anti-trust regulations forced ARCO to sell off many gas stations and truck stops, most of them Sinclair branded. Earl Holding purchased what remained of the Sinclair Oil & Refining Co. from ARCO in 1976, expanding his enterprise from a couple of regional truck stops and resorts into a massive oil company with a marketing area covering most of the Rocky Mountain West.

Little America currently operates resorts in Flagstaff, Arizona; San Diego, California; Little America, Wyoming; Cheyenne, Wyoming; Salt Lake City, Utah; and Sun Valley, Idaho.

From a 1930s Lincoln Highway one-stop, to the "World's Largest Gas Station," to a major western U.S. resort hotel operator, the Covey's, the Holding's, and their Little America properties were instrumental in the early development of today's travel plazas. While other truck stops of the early period were focusing on the trucker's trade, and early gas stations serviced auto tourists, "One-Stops" in general, and Little America in particular, were the first generation of America's current Interstate "travel plazas."

IOWA 80 TRUCK STOP

The successor to Little America's earlier claim of being the world's largest gas station and truck stop is Walcott, Iowa's "Iowa 80" truck stop, located on Interstate 80, just like the current Little America. Exiting I-80 at Exit 284, three miles north of Walcott, the Iowa 80 Truck Stop appears. It is currently the largest, and arguably the most famous truck stop in the world. The distance between Iowa 80 and Little America is approximately 1,100 miles.

Iowa 80 owes its existence to one Bill Moon. Moon had served in the Korean War in the 1950s, then had studied chemistry in college after his military discharge. He was living with his wife Carolyn in Kansas City, and was employed as a District Manager for the Standard Oil Co. of Indiana, when in 1963, he was dispatched by Standard to scout for potentially lucrative sites for future truck stops along the burgeoning Interstate Highway System.

Moon stumbled upon a cornfield along the future routing of I-80, three miles north of Walcott, Iowa, that he later dubbed, "The Perfect Spot." After securing rights to the property, ground was broken in the fall of 1963. When the Iowa 80 Truck Stop opened in 1964, it covered 10 acres and consisted of a small truckers' store, a tire bay, a 56-seat restaurant, a few gas and diesel pumps, and a graveled parking lot. The location was leased and operated by Robert and "Blondie" Hoffman.

In short order, an additional six acres were added, then another 35, then another 160. By 1965, Bill Moon, buoyed by the location's phenomenal success thus far, realized that this was indeed "The Perfect Spot" for a truck stop. He and Carolyn assumed operations in 1965, and Moon left his District Manager job at Standard behind.

Years of unparalleled expansion followed, some directly involving Iowa 80, and some involving associated business ventures. Two of the more successful associated endeavors were Truckomatic and CAT Scales.

In 1969, Bill Moon founded Truckomatic automatic truck washing facilities. His innovative truck washing equipment could wash an entire 18-wheeler in minutes, in a manner similar to running the family sedan through the local car wash. Truckomatics were installed in several truck stops that the Moon family enterprises later operated; many were franchised to other truck stop operators. The name was later changed to Truckomat.

In 1977, the first CAT Scale was opened at a Truckomat location in South Holland, Illinois. This innovative weigh scale revolutionized the industry, as it was the first platform scale that could weigh an entire rig, both tractor and trailer, together. From this single scale, an entire new enterprise was born; by 2006, there were nearly 1,000 CAT Scales operating all over the United States.

The '70s saw similar growth for Iowa 80's trucking-related endeavors: I-80 Investments Co. was birthed in the mid-1970s by Bill Moon and his associate, Carroll Feuerbach, who later became President of the CAT Scale Co. That same year, I-80 Investments purchased The Tennessean Truck Stop in Cornersville, Tennessee. Several additional truck stop acquisitions followed: The Marion Truck Plaza in Marion, Illinois, in 1975; The Oak Grove Truck Stop in Oak Grove, Missouri, in the early 1980s; and the Joplin Petro in Joplin, Missouri, in 1987. Additional truck stop acquisitions were made in subsequent years.

Meanwhile, back at Iowa 80, Bill Moon was considering an idea that would later become the signature event that would forever indelibly etch Iowa 80 onto the roadmaps of nearly every trucker in North America—The Walcott Truckers Jamboree.

First held in 1979, the Walcott Truckers Jamboree was envisioned as a two-day, every July, "customer appreciation"-type of event. Truckers would be invited. Truckers would be honored. Trucking industry vendors would display their products, equipment, and accessories. Truckers would polish and proudly

The Kenly 95 truck stop is an East Coast landmark. Originally opened in 1980 as Truckland Truck Stop, in 1982 the facility became a franchisee of Truckstops of America (T/A). The next 22 years saw continued expansion, and in 2004 the facility was purchased by the Iowa 80 Truck Stop organization, and renamed the Kenly 95 Truck Stop, for its location on Interstate 95 at Kenly, North Carolina. Known for its lighthouse tower patterned after North Carolina's Cape Hatteras Lighthouse, it is one of the best-known stops along Interstate 95. Today it operates as a Petro franchise. These photos date from the summer of 2010.

display their rigs to the public. There would be a competitive "show-and-shine" event for customized hot-rod trucks. Bill Moon's small but ever-growing hobby collection of antique trucks would be exhibited. There would be a free barbeque pork meal and soft drinks for truckers, and two days of fun for all attendees.

From 500 pork chops barbequed on four grills in 1979, the Jamboree has grown to about a score of grills and too many thousands of pork chops and pork sandwiches to count. The 30th Anniversary party in 2009 was the largest yet, with 150 vendor exhibits, 82 trucks competing in the "Super Truck Beauty Contest," 200 trucks in the antique truck display, three live bands, two nights worth of fireworks, an abundance of carnival games, a Truckers Olympics contest, a 300-pound cake in the shape of a big rig that served more than 1,000 people, and a concert featuring country music singer Aaron Tippin.

BACKSTORY

Bill Moon purchased Iowa 80 from AMOCO (the rebranded Standard Oil Co.) in 1984, after years of negotiation. A massive expansion program began almost immediately. Private shower facilities, a TV lounge, and laundry facilities, all for truckers only, were included in the reconstruction. A major restaurant expansion was also in the works.

But even all of these improvements weren't enough for Bill Moon and his dedication to the truck drivers of America. Moon had the original truck stop demolished and re-built in the 1991-1994 period, to make way for his newly-planned "travel center." No sooner had the re-building of the original truck stop ceased, when a two-year expansion was begun. The restaurant was expanded to seat 300 people, a 50-foot salad bar was added, the private showers for truckers were expanded, the truckers' store was enlarged, and an 80-seat movie theater screened its first feature. The TV lounge became the "Drivers' Den" featuring leather chairs and a cozy, "just like home" fireplace.

Ever the visionary, Bill Moon sensed that independently owned and operated truck stops and travel plazas would find tough sledding against the newly emerging national truck stop chains such as Pilot, Petro, and Flying J. Thus, in 1991, Iowa 80 became a franchisee of Truckstops of America (T/A), which in 1997 became TravelCenters of America. TravelCenters of America is a national chain currently consisting of approximately 165 travel centers operating in 40 states.

Bill Moon passed on in 1992 at the age of 59. Family members continue to carry on his rich tradition of providing exemplary service for America's truckers, with yet another re-building in 1994, an expansion to the truck servicing facility in 1998 and 2003, and a fuel center expansion in 2000 and again in 2003.

Groundbreaking ceremonies were held in 2003 for Iowa 80's "Trucking Hall of Fame museum," which houses a rotating selection of approximately 100 trucks from the collection of Bill Moon's many dozens of restored antique trucks, which includes the first Mack Model AC ever built.

Currently, Iowa 80 operates the world's largest truck accessories store which stocks more than 50,000 different chrome, lighting, hot-rodding, and replacement parts for almost any diesel truck.

From 10 acres of Iowa cornfield in 1964, to its current configuration of more than 225 acres, Bill Moon's Iowa 80 Truck Stop/Travel Center is the showcase for the current state of the travel plaza industry.

FROM ONE-STOP TO ONE-STOP

What began as a handful of family-operated "one-stops" on a series of mud-holes called The Lincoln Highway and similar named composites of farm-to-market roads in the first decades of the 20th century, has reached its zenith with near Las Vegas-like glitz and glitter of the Iowa 80 Truck Stop on I-80. And just as I-80 has become today's version of the Lincoln Highway, the Iowa 80 Truck Stop similarly emulates and updates the original "one-stops" that gave birth and re-birth to the auto/truck stops that permeate today's Interstate Highway travel.

CHAPTER 3
OIL COMPANY-BRANDED TRUCK STOPS: PROFILES OF BRANDS

Today's truck stops are operated similar to a chain-store model, in that one company owns and operates numerous outlets under one brand, or because of several industry mergers, various brands. It wasn't always that way, however. For most of the twentieth century, actual ownership of truck stops was in the hands of individual operators. These operators were assisted in developing a common brand and image by the company that supplied their petroleum products. Most oil companies market only in certain regions, and often the truck stops that they branded were the most distant outlets from the core of their operations. Only two oil companies, TEXACO and Phillips, reached the point of branded marketing in all 50 states, but during the late 1960s and early 1970s several others, notably AMOCO and affiliates, EXXON and affiliates, GULF, Mobil, and Shell, came close.

Most major oil companies and their affiliates were involved in branding truck stops to some extent. Companies such as PURE and Skelly built up extensive networks by seeking out and rebranding sites formerly branded by other companies, and by providing financing to successful service station dealers and truck stop operators to allow them to relocate or expand their facilities. Often, through financial arrangements, the supplying oil company retained control of a site without having to operate the location directly. Other oil companies set up truck stop programs within their overall marketing plans, each differing to some degree in depth. Early leaders in developing a truck stop network include GULF, Sinclair, and AMOCO affiliate Pan-Am. As their branded networks expanded, supplying oil companies would set up credit card exchanges with companies with which they were unlikely to compete, such as companies outside of their core marketing areas. These credit card exchanges allowed truckers to make loyal use of one company's credit card coast-to-coast.

A limited number of companies operated truck stops directly. Many smaller oil companies and jobbers for major companies might own and operate a site that they considered to be a truck stop. In some cases, these sites were simply strategically located service stations that also sold diesel fuel. With others, there was a deliberate effort to emulate truck stops that were part of the programs of large oil companies. Some independent gasoline marketers such as Site and Martin built locations that were specifically designed to be truck stops. Many operated on the "honor all" credit card system, common to discount gas station operators of the 1950s through the early 1970s, wherein a station had private account arrangements to accept all major oil credit cards. In later years this type of operation has become dominant, in that Pilot, Flying J, Petro and others are company-owned and operated; indeed, Pilot began as a traditional independent gasoline discounter.

"Mom & Pop" comprised an even smaller final category, often operating only a single outlet, or perhaps a pair, if the original location had proven to be particularly successful. Most, but not all of these Mom & Pops, were tied to a major oil company, but operated their truck stop (or their small chain) within the confines of the truck stop "network" with which they were affiliated. Usually, the only obligation Mom & Pop had to an oil company was contractual: the purchase and sale of branded fuels. The oil company had no say in how the truck stop was operated. As such, Mom & Pop could easily change brands at the end of a contract, if a more lucrative deal could be reached with a competing oil company. It was through this avenue that many regional oil companies lost truck stops to larger oil companies.

This chapter attempts to sketch a corporate profile for many of the oil company brands that have appeared at truck stops. This list is by no means 100% complete, but it does cover nearly all of the major players in these categories.

"Number of confirmed branded truck stops" refers to truck stops that were confirmed as operating during the year listed as cited by dated truck stop listings or directories issued by the individual oil company in question, or by oil company or truck stop industry trade publications; in certain instances totals listed were gathered from other oil companies' publications with which the company in question maintained credit card exchanges. Following the oil company listings are brief histories of today's companies that are specific truck stop operators, along with some information about truck stop organizations and the history of three key travel stop operators of yesterday.

AMOCO and Affiliates

American Oil Company and Standard Oil Co. of Indiana

CORPORATE

• The company we think of today as AMOCO was founded in 1889 as Standard Oil Company of Indiana, the domestic refining and midwestern U.S. marketing division of the old Standard Oil Trust. Their first gasoline brand name was Red Crown.

• After the 1911 breakup of the Standard Oil Trust, Standard expanded from its original marketing territory with the purchase of several existing operations. In 1925 Standard purchased Pan American Petroleum (Pan-Am), an international, integrated oil company with marketing in New England and the southern U.S., with a minority interest in Baltimore-based American Oil Company.

• American Oil was founded by Louis and Jacob Blaustein in 1910. The company began as a kerosene distributor, but by 1915 was refining and marketing their benzol-blended "Amoco-Gas." They built a small chain of company-owned "Lord Baltimore" gas stations in Baltimore and Washington DC, and expanded their distribution through the rest of Maryland, as well as into Pennsylvania, Delaware, Virginia and West Virginia. In 1923, the Blausteins contracted with Pan-Am for crude oil supply that would, by 1933, in a complex stock arrangement, give Pan-Am control of American Oil.

• In the 1920s Standard also expanded west, with the purchase of Midwest Oil and Arro Oil and Refining, which they consolidated into Utah Oil Refining.

• During 1933-1934 there was extensive marketing realignment, after which the AMOCO name could be found from Maine to Florida, the Pan-Am name in Alabama, Tennessee, Mississippi and Louisiana, the Standard brand in the company's original assigned 14 Midwest states, and Utah Oil's "Vico" brand (UTOCO by 1946) in Utah and Idaho.

• Standard of Indiana purchased Standard of Nebraska in 1939, consolidating the Standard name in 15 states.

• In 1954 Standard's Pan-Am subsidiary purchased the remaining portion of American Oil and the division was reorganized as American Oil. AMOCO began replacing the Pan-Am brand on gas stations in the southern U.S. in 1956.

• On December 31, 1960, all of Standard of Indiana's domestic marketing was reorganized into a subsid-

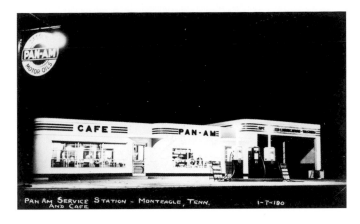

Pan-Am was the first of the Standard of Indiana divisions to become involved in truck stops. The effort began in the late 1930s with a series of Pan-Am stations that included larger parking areas and cafés. This photo is the oldest example that we've seen, and was taken in Monteagle, Tennessee, about 1940.

Another early photo of one of the Pan-Am café stations, direct predecessors to Pan-Am's truck stop network. This location was photographed in Attalla, Alabama, in about 1940.

Moore's Pan-Am truck stop was opened in July of 1954 and was one of the last of the smaller Pan-Am truck stops to be constructed. This location was on U.S. 61 South in Cleveland, Mississippi, and was photographed at the time of the opening.

In the mid-1950s Pan-Am developed a much larger prototype for their truck stop network. One operator built at least three of these facilities, featuring the large center tower with clock and called, logically, The Clock Truck Stop. This location was on U.S. 45 south of Selmer, Tennessee. Others could be found in Picayune, Mississippi, and Oneonta, Alabama.

By the middle 1950s Pan-Am had incorporated larger restaurant facilities into their truck stops. This Alabama example features the restaurant area prominently, with open service bays, high enough for trucks, located at the rear of the facility.

In 1956 a new façade design was developed for Pan-Am truck stops, and that design carried over into the era when the AMOCO brand replaced Pan-Am, beginning in 1958. The new design was also adapted to the existing truck stop design with the central tower, as you will see when you compare this building with the Selmer, Tennessee, location seen elsewhere in this book. This location was one of a chain called "The Torch" truck stops and is located at the junction of U.S. 29 and U.S. 80 just east of Tuskegee, Alabama. This facility is still standing, though is no longer a truck stop. Other "The Torch" truck stops were found in Atmore, Alabama, and at Collins and Petal, Mississippi.

Other truck stops sold Pan-Am products (later AMOCO and American), but were not built to specific company designs. One such location is the TK Truck Stop on U.S. 31 just north of Athens, Alabama. This photo shows the TK Truck Stop shortly after the Pan-Am brand was changed to American in 1961.

iary that was named, coincidently, American Oil. The American name was introduced to replace AMOCO in the eastern and southern portions of the U.S., as well as UTOCO marketing areas in the western U.S. The Standard name would be retained on stations in the Midwest. The American Oil subsidiary would be renamed AMOCO Oil Company in 1971. The AMOCO brand would replace American, beginning in 1974 and would be optionally used in the Standard marketing territory beginning at this time.

• In 1985 Standard Oil Co. of Indiana was renamed to the AMOCO Corporation. This corporate structure would remain in place until 1998, when AMOCO merged with British Petroleum (BP). Stations would remain AMOCO (and optionally Standard, in the Midwest) until 2001, when the BP brand began replacing both AMOCO and Standard.

Truck Stop Operations
• AMOCO's truck stop marketing began in the 1940s in the southern U.S., when their Pan-Am subsidiary began working with their jobber and dealer network to site truck stops at strategic locations in the South.

From a modest start in the 1930s, Slim Olson's Truck Stop was enlarged into what was, at the time, claimed to be the world's largest service station, selling Pep 88 and later UTOCO products through 43 pumps. As the fame of the site grew, Slim Olson signage took greater precedence over oil company branding. The first scene dates from about 1940, the later from about 1950. The facility was located on U.S. 91, at 2301 S. Main St. in Bountiful, Utah.

Location was often the key to making a truck stop successful. In the 1930s, Rife Brothers opened a Pep 88 station on U.S. 89 at the intersection that makes up Mount Carmel Junction, Utah. Over the years the location was expanded, and progressed as the oil company did, through the Pep 88, UTOCO, American, and finally AMOCO brands. The first photo dates from the late 1940s; the second, with the company's UTOCO sign a much larger feature, dates from about 1958. The third photo shows an enlarged station displaying the American brand, introduced in 1961. Though barely more than a service station, directories from the 1960s list this as a truck stop. In later years Shell and the TEXACO products were sold here.

Within a few years the Pan-Am brand was found on numerous truck stops in the southern U.S.
• There was some localized branding of truck stops by the AMOCO, Standard and UTOCO divisions in the 1950s. After Pan-Am and AMOCO came under full corporate ownership and were consolidated, uniform truck stop signage began to appear at sites operated under all four brands. When all domestic marketing was consolidated as American Oil in 1960, the truck stop program went into high gear, presenting a uniform image and product range coast to coast.
• *Number of confirmed branded truck stops and significant marketing strategies, by year:*
1960: 69 AMOCO branded truck stops were operating in the U.S., from Louisiana and Arkansas in the south, up the Atlantic seaboard to Maine.
1961: 227 American/Standard branded truck stops were operating in the U.S., from Maine in the east, to Kennewick, Washington in the west.
1963: 236 American/Standard branded truck stops were operating in the U.S.
1964-5: 248 American/Standard branded truck stops were operating in the U.S.

In the late 1940s, other Slim Olson's stations were opened at Elko and Winnemucca, Nevada. This location, on U.S. 40 about a mile west of Elko, was at the time Nevada's largest station, with 23 pumps; another example where oversized service stations functioned as truck stops before the concept was fully developed. When AMOCO, Pan-Am, Standard, and UTOCO organized their truck stop organization in the late 1950s, Slim Olson's sites were included.

Fote's UTOCO Truck Stop was located at 413 S. 2nd West in Salt Lake City, Utah. Despite being an "in town" truck stop, the site advertises parking for up to 50 trucks. This photo dates from about 1948.

1966: 237 American/Standard branded truck stops were operating in the U.S.
1967: 219 American/Standard branded truck stops were operating in the U.S.
1968: 224 American/Standard branded truck "plazas" were operating in the U.S. (having changed from the 1967 "truck stop" nomenclature).
1971: A re-designed logo was introduced concurrent to the re-institution of the AMOCO name at the corporate level.

One of the oldest corporate-type truck stop photos included in this book is this photo of Becker Brothers' Truck Terminal, which was selling AMOCO products in this 1939 photograph. It is believed that this facility was in the Richmond, Virginia, area.

McClenny's Truck Stop operated for many years along U.S. Hwy. 58, just west of Suffolk, Virginia. This photo dates from the summer of 1959.

By the time this 1965 photo was taken, McClenny's Truck Stop had rebranded from Amoco to American. American Oil products were sold here into the middle 1970s, although the brandname would revert to Amoco in 1974.

Marvin and Ruth's Truckers Paradise was one of many truck stops located along U.S. 17 just south of Savannah, Georgia. Although the facility appears to be little more than the typical AMOCO station of the era, advertisements mentioned that they offer three acres of parking, bunk and shower facilities, and of course a restaurant and 24-hour service. This photo dates from about 1950.

Until replaced by Interstate 95, U.S. Hwy.1 was the main north-south highway connecting the East Coast's major cities, and as such, was a major trucking route, with truck stops strategically located from Maine to Florida. The creatively named Trux Top was located on U.S.1 at Ashland, Virginia, and is seen here as it appeared in the summer of 1959.

One of the AMOCO division's largest truck stops in the pre-1961 era was the AMOCO Turnpike Service, on Ohio Route 7, four miles south of Youngstown. A large rooftop sign, originally displaying the AMOCO oval, welcomed truckers to the facility. After the American brand replaced AMOCO, the huge sign was modified to a torch and oval design, but kept the AMOCO name. This photo dates from 1963.

Breezewood, Pennsylvania, has been a key interchange on the Pennsylvania Turnpike since the road opened in October of 1939. In 1941, The Gateway Inn, one of the first businesses to cater to tourists in Breezewood, was opened by Merle and Marion Snyder. In the early years they sold ESSO products, operated a restaurant, and offered rooms to truckers. Later on, AMOCO (and even later, American) products were sold here, as seen in the photo from about 1970. In 1956 the Snyder's Nephew, Frank Bittner and his wife, Alice, took over management of the site. Today the location has been rebuilt on the original site and operates as a T/A travel center and Valero gas station.

1974: Standard of Indiana rebranded all of their American outlets and many of their Standard outlets back to the AMOCO brand.

1976-7: 244 AMOCO branded truck plazas were operating in the U.S. AMOCO had partnered with a network of 88 western U.S. outlets selling diesel fuel operated by Chevron (another oil company with ties to the original Standard Oil Trust) to create a network of 335 truck plazas. These AMOCO and Chevron truck stops were tied together by a shared "Transicard" credit card system.

1999: AMOCO merged with British Petroleum to become BP/AMOCO.

The Cross Country Truck Terminal and Restaurant was one of the new truck stop facilities of the 1960s that operated under the American brand. It was located at the junction of Interstate 4 and U.S. 27 in Haines City, Florida, and was photographed here in about 1970.

Fossland's began life as a roadside restaurant along U.S. 41, just on the Illinois side of the Illinois-Wisconsin state line. Standard products were sold here for many years. More of a road house than a truck stop, its location and variety of amenities made it a popular stop for truckers anyway.

Standard of Indiana expanded the American brand coast-to-coast, with only the 15 states where they still held the rights to the Standard name exempted from the 1961 change. As part of the expansion, American purchased some of the former El Paso properties in Arizona and New Mexico in 1964. This truck stop was selling American products on Interstate 10 at Fort Grant Rd. in Willcox, Arizona, when photographed in 1970.

The crossroads city of Bloomington, Illinois, has been home to a number of truck stops throughout the past 75 years. One of the largest was Streids, selling Standard products and offering a large restaurant and truck service. This photo dates from about 1959.

Bud's M&M Truck Stop, selling Standard products, is typical of many Rocky Mountain truck stops of the 1950s. There is a lot of open space, albeit a gravel lot, with fuel islands up front, service to the back of the lot, and a restaurant at one end of the property. This photo dates from about 1958.

In 1948 Fred Bosselman and brother-in-law Al Eaton opened a Standard branded truck stop on U.S. 30 just east of Grand Island, Nebraska. The first photo dates from about 1950. In the 1950s the original site was enlarged, as is seen in the later 1960 photo. This truck stop also operated as a large truck parts store and repair facility. It remains in operation today.

In 1965, after Interstate 80 was completed around Grand Island, Nebraska, Fred Bosselman opened a second truck stop at the U.S. 281 interchange. Today, with various family members involved, Bosselmans operates eight truck stops and are franchised by Pilot and Sinclair.

The Parkway Café and Standard Service was operating as a truck stop of sorts along U.S. 30 in Lexington, Nebraska. The first photo dates from 1959, while the later one dates from about 1965.

During the 1960s, Standard of Indiana developed a very functional two-story layout for their truck stops, with locations being built in this pattern throughout America's heartland. This site is the Stop One Truck Stop on Interstate 70 and Indiana Route 1 in Cambridge City, Indiana. This photo dates from about 1968.

Another of Standards "standardized" truck stops was Greenwood Truck Stop on Interstate 80 at Greenwood, Nebraska. This photo dates from about 1968.

The Triangle Truck Stop and Helen's Café was located on Interstate 70 at U.S. 40 in Wakeeney, Kansas. It was one of a network of truck stops that Standard of Indiana built throughout their marketing area in the 1960s.

Rural Standard truck stop on U.S. 67 at Coldwater, Missouri, circa 1970.

Iowa 80 Truck Stop began as a Standard truck stop in 1964. Located on Interstate 80 at Walcott, Iowa, this scene shows the facility in the late 1980s.

ASHLAND and Affiliates
Ashland Oil Company (Branded Marketing)
CORPORATE
• Founded in 1924 as a refining division of Swiss Oil Co. Gasoline was marketed under the brand name "Pepper."
• Ashland Oil absorbed Swiss Oil in about 1935. In 1946 the Ashland brand name was introduced to replace the former Pepper brand.
• Between 1950 and 1982, Ashland absorbed several smaller regional oil companies including: Aetna Oil Co.; Frontier Refining; National Refining (White Rose); Freedom–Valvoline Oil Company (Freedom Oil Works and Valvoline oil had merged in 1943); Payless Oil Co.; Northwest Refining (SuperAmerica); Red Head Oil Co.; Oskey Bros. Oil Co.(North Star); Southern Oil Company of New York (Rotary); Hi-Fy Oil Co.; Fleet (Hood Oil Co.); and Tresler Oil Co. (Comet).
• Marketing went through several consolidations. By 1960 the Ashland name had replaced Aetna, Frontier, and White Rose. Valvoline had phased out gasoline marketing prior to its merger with Ashland Oil, in favor of lubricant manufacturing.
• Later purchases were operated under their individual brand names until they were phased out in the 1980s. Sites that could be converted to convenience stores were kept and rebranded SuperAmerica, which became a corporate-wide convenience store trademark in the 1980s. Of these operations it is known that Oskey Brothers and Tresler owned or branded truck stops and SuperAmerica operated some sites that they labeled as truck stops.
• Many of Ashland's western Pennsylvania stations were sold to SUNOCO in about 1985.
• Ashland Oil's refining and marketing operations were merged with Marathon's in 1998 to form Marathon Ashland Petroleum. In 2005 Marathon purchased Ashland's portion of the combined operation and began phasing out the Ashland brand name. SuperAmerica sites in all states except Minnesota and Wisconsin were rebranded to Marathon's Speedway name.

Truck Stop Operations
• *Number of confirmed Ashland branded truck stops operating in the U.S.:* Approximately one half-dozen Ashland branded truck stops have been confirmed, all having operated between 1960 and 1984.

Typical of the First Generation truck stop was the White House Truck Stop, selling Ashland products on Route 2 near Steelton, West Virginia. This photo dates from about 1957.

Ashland Oil Co. Subsidiaries:
• *Tresler Oil Co.*—Tresler Oil operated between five and 10 truck stops in Ohio, Kentucky and Tennessee. This effort began with the opening of their Cincinnati riverfront site in 1950 known as The Speedcenter.
• *Oskey Brothers Petroleum*—Oskey Brothers branded some sites that were classified as truck stops. These locations dated from the 1960s and operated under their North Star brand.
• *SuperAmerica*—SuperAmerica was founded in 1961 and by the middle 1960s was a large general merchandise convenience store operator. Ashland Oil purchased Northwestern Refining and their SuperAmerica operation in 1970. Eventually the SuperAmerica brand was imported into other c-store operations owned or operated by Ashland Oil. In the

In the 1960s, Cincinnati based Tresler Oil Co. began to build a string of truck stops along Interstate 75 in Ohio, Kentucky, and Tennessee. The southernmost location was in Knoxville, Tennessee, and is shown here in about 1975.

course of these various consolidations, the SuperAmerica brand was applied to various sites that were considered to be truck stops. In addition, the SuperAmerica division began building a network of truck stops in the 1990s that were rebranded as Speedway truck stops after the Marathon-Ashland merger.

Atlantic Richfield
Atlantic Refining Co.
• Founded by Charles Lockhart in Philadelphia in 1866 as Atlantic Petroleum Storage Co. The name was changed to Atlantic Refining Co. in 1870.
• Strictly an East Coast marketer, with gas stations from New Hampshire to Florida. Marketed as far west as eastern Ohio and into Tennessee around Bristol.
• In 1965, Atlantic began talks of a merger with the PURE Oil Co., but terminated them due to Atlantic and PURE being direct competitors in several marketing areas.
• In 1965, Atlantic, operating stations along the eastern seaboard, began merger talks with the Richfield Oil Corp. of California. Atlantic and Richfield merged in January, 1966, and from then until 1970, operated as separate companies on their respective coasts.
• Atlantic Richfield's 1969-70 merger with Sinclair hastened the introduction of the ARCO brand name, which had been under consideration for several years.

Triple O Service and Supply was primarily a truck parts and service facility that added fuel sales (Atlantic) and a restaurant to become a more complete truck stop. This photo dates from the early 1950s. In the PURE Truck Stop expansion beginning in the late 1950s, this facility would be rebranded PURE, as is seen in a photo elsewhere in this book.

Chino Valley Truck Stop was located on U.S. 89 at Chino Valley, Arizona. It was owned and operated by Eric and Lillian Hagstedt, and existed as an example of a Second Generation truck stop. Richfield (California) products were sold, and the café advertised home cooked meals and pastries. It is seen here as it appeared in about 1960.

Dinty's Café, motel and service station was listed as an official Richfield truck stop during the early 1960s. Founded in 1918, the original building was constructed on a site where the rock cliff was cut away to allow construction. During the 1930s the café added a TEXACO station, which later was rebranded to Richfield, as seen in this 1962 photo. Located on U.S. 30-97 at Biggs Junction, Oregon, during the 1960s it was operated by Mr. and Mrs. P.L. Finley. Dinty's is still in operation today, although the original buildings have all been replaced.

In 1970 the ARCO brand replaced both Atlantic and Richfield, and rebranding began in certain markets at Sinclair stations, as well.
• In 1973 ARCO began divesting itself of Sinclair holdings to various entities. In 1976, the remaining portions of Sinclair were sold to independent marketer Earl Holding, owner of the Little America Resorts chain, and son-in-law of LARCO's S. M. Covey. Today's Sinclair Oil is a result of that purchase, and the brand is found in the Midwest and Rocky Mountain West.

• In the 1980s ARCO withdrew completely from marketing on the East Coast. At that time an independent marketing company was formed by some former ARCO executives who then reintroduced the Atlantic name. In 1988, the new Atlantic was sold to SUNOCO, and all operations were eventually rebranded to the SUNOCO brand by the mid-1990s due to marketing overlap of some 1,000 gas stations in Pennsylvania and New York.

Truck Stop Operations
• *Number of confirmed Atlantic branded truck stops operating in the U.S.:*
1958: 28
1960: 30
1961: 33
1962: 40
1965: 58
1966: 70
1967: 71
1970: All Atlantic and Richfield truck stops rebranded to ARCO. The 70-plus Atlantic truck stops combined with more than 30 Richfield truck stops would have put ARCO's totals at over 100 during their first year under the brand. Large portions of the ARCO network were abandoned within a few years, leaving about 40 truck stops by the late 1970s and 30 or so in the 1970s. Most of the Sinclair truck stop network never made the transition to ARCO.

Richfield Oil Co. of California
• Founded in California in about 1901 from the holdings of the Petroleum Products Co. of California and the Rio Grande Petroleum Co., both of which very little history is known.
• West Coast retail marketing of gasoline began in about 1915.
• East Coast retail marketing began in about 1929 after Richfield established the Richfield Oil Co. of New York through the purchases of New York City's Walburn Petroleum Co. and Acewood Petroleum Co.
• During The Depression, heavy investment by the Cities Service Co. and the Sinclair Oil Co. saved Richfield from bankruptcy. During this time, Sinclair took over Richfield Oil Co. of New York as a wholly-owned marketing subsidiary.
• Richfield merged with the Atlantic Refining Co. in 1966, and later with Sinclair, to form the Atlantic Richfield Oil Co. (ARCO).

Truck Stop Operations
• *Number of confirmed Richfield Oil Co. of California branded truck stops operating in the U.S. by year:*
1960: 16
1966: 33
1967: 26
1968: 30
1970: 99 (See notes about the consolidated company in the Atlantic Refining section above.)

British Petroleum and Affiliates
BP USA
• Founded in England in 1901 by William D'Arcy.
• Became involved in North American petroleum marketing in 1958, when BP established 400 gas stations in Quebec and Ontario, Canada.
• The BP brand first appeared in the United States when the company acquired nearly 9,700 Sinclair gas stations, located in states from Maine to Florida, in 1969. Atlantic Richfield had agreed to sell these locations in order to receive U.S. Justice Department approval of the merger of Atlantic Richfield with Sinclair. In 1973, BP sold their company-owned locations and jobber contracts in the southern U.S. to American Petrofina (FINA).
• In 1970 BP acquired a 51 percent (controlling) interest in The Standard Oil Co. of Ohio (SOHIO). They acquired the remaining interests in the mid-1980s, making SOHIO completely British-owned. SOHIO's name was changed to BP America at the time of the acquisition.
• In 1989, BP decided to eliminate all of their other brand names, and convert all interests to the BP brand, beginning the following year. Up until that time the BP brand had diminished greatly in scope, but could be found at a limited number of locations from Virginia north to New England, either on company-operated pumpers or at jobber-supplied portions of the old Sinclair network. Some BP jobbers, particularly in Virginia, West Virginia, Maryland, and Pennsylvania, were using the Boron brand.
• Brands converted to BP included SOHIO and its affiliates, specifically Boron, Wm. Penn, and Gas–N-Go; the GULF brand outlets (and jobber contracts)

in the Carolinas, Georgia, Florida, Alabama, Mississippi, Tennessee and Kentucky which BP had purchased in 1985; and all West Coast Mobil stations which BP had also purchased in the late 1980s. Prior to the BP conversion, the GULF and Mobil brands had been licensed to BP for use in these states for a limited period of time.

• In 1999, BP merged with AMOCO (Standard Oil Co. of Indiana) to become BP/AMOCO. AMOCO outlets were converted to the BP brand in 2001.

• In April, 2000, BP/AMOCO purchased Atlantic Richfield. Atlantic Richfield's ARCO brand remains in use as of this writing.

Truck Stop Operations

• With the 1969 purchase of Sinclair stations in the east, the BP brand first appeared on truck stops that were formerly part of the Sinclair network in that region. Much of that network was disassembled within a few years of the rebranding. The BP name was not added to any truck stops (other than perhaps on a local rebranding basis) until the general rebranding in 1990.

• During the 1980s Truckstops of America (T/A) was purchased by BP America. Fuels sold at some of the T/A sites had been branded Boron. Following the BP AMOCO merger, truck stops in the former AMOCO/Standard network were rebranded to BP.

Champlin and Affiliates

Champlin Refining Co.

• Founded by H. H. Champlin sometime before 1920, Champlin's first gas station opened in 1923 in Enid, Oklahoma. Hundreds of Champlin branded gas stations were in operation throughout the Midwest by the advent of WWII.

• H. H. Champlin died in 1944. Son Joe assumed presidency in 1943. Joe died in San Diego, California, in 1970.

• The company was sold to The Chicago Corp. in 1954.

• Venezuela's government-owned oil organization purchased Champlin in about 1984, and the retail marketing division was sold off to American Petrofina (FINA). The FINA brand replaced Champlin that same year.

The Seventy One Truck Stop was located, logically, along Highway 71 at Diamond, Missouri. Typical of rural truck stops in the Midwest, this stop featured a large lot, restaurant, and repair facilities. Champlin products were being sold here when this photograph was taken in about 1968.

Truck Stop Operations

• Prior to 1960, several Champlin branded jobbers were operating truck stops as part of their network of outlets. In 1961 the company took notice of the jobber efforts and began offering assistance in the development of truck stops. Within five years Champlin's network of Food and Fuel Plazas could be found throughout the Midwest.

The Champlin Café was located on U.S. 30 east of Columbus, Nebraska, and is typical of the type of truck stop developed by Champlin jobbers in the Great Plains states. This photo dates from about 1959.

In the early 1960s, Champlin developed standardized layouts for truck stops and used them for both company and jobber stations throughout the midwestern states. This example was a new construction in the summer of 1966, and was located in Yankton, South Dakota.

Chevron and Affiliates

Standard Oil Co. of California

• Isaac Blake, who founded CONOCO, was involved in the creation of Pacific Coast Oil Co., which later became Standard of California.

• Created by the merger of California Star Oil Works and a group of investors, Pacific Coast Oil Co.—a direct Chevron predecessor—was founded on September 10, 1879. Pacific Coast merged with Standard Oil Co. of Iowa in 1900. The merger was re-structured in 1906, and the newly created entity dropped the Pacific Coast name and became Standard Oil Co. of California.

• After the 1911 government-mandated breakup of Standard Oil, Standard of California was assigned production, refining, and retail marketing in the far western U.S.

• Standard of California is credited with operating one of the very first retail gasoline stations, opened at the company's bulk plant in Seattle in 1907.

• The company began to construct a West Coast network of gas stations in 1915, and originally marketed gasoline in California, Oregon, Washington, Idaho, Nevada, Arizona, and Utah.

• Standard of California was one of the first compa-

Standard Oil Co. of Texas, a subsidiary of Standard of California, was supplying this truck stop at 3300 N. Chadbourne St. in San Angelo, Texas, when photographed here about 1955. The "Chevron Truck Station" signage was unique to dealer-operated truck stops supplied by all of the western Standard of California subsidiaries.

nies to create a chain of look-alike gas stations from a single design prototype.

• In the early 1930s, Standard Oil Co. of California expanded into the Rocky Mountain and Great Plains states by opening an office in Denver. This operation was known as The California Company and branded jobbers and dealers under the Calso name. Op-

Standard Oil Co. of California introduced their Calso brand into eastern marketing areas in late 1945, eventually building a jobber network from Maine to Virginia, then rebranding the operation in 1959 to Chevron. Johnny's Truck Stop and Diner on U.S. 22 west of Clinton, New Jersey, was selling Chevron products when photographed here in about 1965.

erations were also established in El Paso, Texas. The new entity was named "Pasotex," which later became Standard Oil Co. of Texas.

• At this time, Standard of California utilized a red, white and blue color scheme in their home territory and in the Standard of Texas territory. The California Company used a green, blue, and white color scheme in its Rocky Mountain marketing territory—with stations named "Calso" to help differentiate it from other Standard Oil companies.

• In 1945, all Calso operations in the Rocky Moun-

tain states were rebranded to "Chevron," along with all dealer-operated stations in the Standard of California and Standard of Texas territories, with Chevron stations using a maroon, green and cream color scheme.

• In 1946 Standard of California established an East Coast operation known as the California Oil Co., which adopted the Calso name that was being phased out in the Rocky Mountain West. The Calso name was changed to Chevron in 1959. Marketing in this operation extended from Maine south to Virginia.

• Chevron purchased Standard Oil of Kentucky ("Kyso") in 1961. The Standard name was retained in their five-state marketing area until 1977.

• Chevron purchased GULF Oil Co. in 1984. GULF in the southeast was sold to BP, which in turn rebranded the GULF network in 1990 to BP. GULF in the northeast was sold to convenience store operator Cumberland Farms, which has maintained the brand ever since, and, after purchasing nationwide rights to the GULF name in 2009, has begun expanding back into the southeastern states.

• In 1984, Chevron officially changed their name to the Chevron Corp.

Truck Stop Operations

• In the late 1940s Standard of California established the brand "Chevron Truck Station" and began assembling a network of these dealer- and jobber-operated sites in the West, including the Rocky Mountain and

Chevron operated a series of "truck stations" in its native West Coast territory, including the Los Angeles Truck Terminal, shown here in the middle 1960s.

Standard of Texas territories. Chevron truck stops were also in operation in the Northeastern Calso territory. Standard Oil Company of Kentucky branded a large number of independently owned and operated truck stops in their five-state southeastern territory, as well.

Highway 17 south of Savannah was home to numerous truck stops, including many which appear in this book. Among the various locations along this major thoroughfare was DeSoto Truck Terminal. A modern steel structure with brick accents housed a restaurant and truckers' store, and a truck parts business, while service was relegated to a separate building. Standard Oil of Kentucky (later Chevron) products were sold here. This photo dates from about 1964.

On U.S. 301 just south of Jesup, Georgia, Hoke's was an unusual truck stop in that multiple brands of fuel were being sold. Pumps for the Standard Oil of Kentucky and Colonial Oil Co. (of Florida) brands are shown in this photo, and advertising indicates that PURE products were sold here, as well. In another unusual twist, the facility raised its own quail for a quail dinner special offered by the restaurant. In an appeal to out-of-state truckers, special signage points out that ESSO credit cards are honored, which attracted ESSO customers, as ESSO did not market in Georgia at the time this photo was taken in about 1962.

CITGO

Cities Service Oil Co.

• Henry L. Doherty created Cities Service in 1910, as a public utility company, operating natural gas, lighting, ice delivery, and streetcar services in Tulsa, Oklahoma.

• Cities Service began petroleum marketing in about 1914 and operated service stations throughout the East and Midwest.

• In 1954, Cities Service obtained exclusive rights to operate service stations on the New Jersey Turnpike.

• In 1965, Cities Service introduced CITGO as a new brandname for their gasoline, and unveiled a new CITGO logo in white, blue, and shaded reds, replacing a green and white "expanding circle and delta" logo created in 1946, that dated to 1910 in a black and white incarnation.

• In 1983, CITGO was purchased by The Southland Corp., operators of the 7-11 Convenience Store chain.

• In about 1984, CITGO was purchased by the government-owned Petrofina PDVSA Corp. of Venezuela, who also purchased Champlin at approximately the same time.

Truck Stop Operations

Cities Service made no apparent attempt to build a truck stop network, but it is known that there were

Two Chiefs Truck Stop is a great example of where a strategically located service station expanded into a truck stop simply by adding a restaurant and diesel fuel. Located on U.S. 98 in Panama City, Florida, it served truckers on what was then a major east-west highway. Standard Oil of Kentucky products were being sold here when this photo was taken in the mid 1960s.

The Skillet was a Cities Service branded truck stop and restaurant along U.S. 66 in Rolla, Missouri. Reportedly, the facility started as a simple service station, then later added a café that became locally quite famous. Its location along U.S. 66 made the facility a natural for a truck stop, and it functioned as such for many years. This photo dates from 1958.

A restaurant and service station has occupied the corner of U.S. 54 and 150 in Farmer City, Illinois, for many years. In the older scene the facility is known as Carl's Truck Stop and was selling Cities Service products. It was a rare example of a farmhouse type truck stop more common in the late 1930s, although this photo dates from about 1955. In the later photo the name has been changed to Grier's Restaurant and Motor Stop and it appears that additional fueling positions have been added in the front of the lot. The later photo dates from about 1960.

Dean Powers was the Diamond T truck dealer in Cedar Rapids, Iowa. He expanded his dealership by later adding trailer sales, and full service truck stop facilities, selling Cities Service products. This photo shows the facility in the middle 1950s.

Cities Service branded truck stops scattered throughout their marketing area by the early WWII era. CITGO today operates almost exclusively as a jobber supplier; numerous CITGO jobbers operate truck stops today.

• *Number of confirmed CITGO branded truck stops operating in the U.S.:* Fewer than two dozen Cities Service/CITGO branded truck stops have been confirmed.

From the 1930s through the 1960s, many existing businesses found themselves positioned, by benefit of location, to add truck stop facilities to their existing business mix. Smith Brothers Oil Co. was one such facility. Smith Brothers served as a Cities Service distributor, operated a restaurant, and sold International trucks and Desoto and Plymouth autos. The existing fuel, restaurant, and truck service facilities made the location an ideal truck stop. They were located on U.S. 301 just south of Sylvania, Georgia and this photo dates from about 1952.

The Rainbow Inn truck stop and restaurant was located on U.S. 78 just east of Anniston, Alabama, and sold Cities Service products for many years. Operated by Mr. and Mrs. Charles Knight, the facility advertised good food 24 hours a day and three motels adjacent to the lot. This photo appears to be from the early 1940s. Note the arching "Rainbow Inn" signage over the entrance to the café, at right.

In this later 1940s photo, The Rainbow Inn now sports an extension on its pump island yardarm signage that advertises "Under New Management" and a declaration that they are now "Open 24 Hours." It appears that the original clapboard-sided structures at center have now been re-sided with brick, or faux-brick, and that there has been an additional structure constructed behind the fuel pumps. The original "Rainbow Inn" arched signage still adorns the entrance to the café. At right can be seen an early-1950s Chevrolet or GMC Cannonball car hauler.

Fortmeyer's was perhaps the largest Cities Service truck stop ever built. Located on Goshen Rd. at Interstate 69 in Fort Wayne, Indiana, the complex consisted of more than 30 acres of parking, along with truck service facilities, restaurant, Cities Service products, with various motels adjacent. The oldest of the three photos shows the site while still carrying the Cities Service brand, circa 1965, while the later two photos show the site in the late 1960s under the CITGO brand. A restaurant and CITGO station still occupy this location today.

Davis Cross Roads Café was operating in Salina, Kansas, in the early 1950s. Both automobile and truck traffic was solicited.

Dick's Place, on U.S. 360 at Amelia, Virginia, is typical of rural truck stops of the 1960s. The building is a prefabricated steel structure, and most functions of the truck stop were handled under one roof. This stop featured a 24-hour restaurant, accessory store, showers, scales, and a barber shop. They were selling Cities Service products when photographed here in 1965.

The Indiana Toll Road opened in 1956 and featured eight pairs of service plazas. Cities Service operated the Governor Henry Schricker and Governor George Craig plazas at the Elkhard interchange during the 1950s and 1960s. Due to the limited access nature of toll roads, and the food and fuel facilities offered at the service plazas, these served as de facto truck stops, although built primarily to cater to automobile travel. This photo shows the Cities Service facilities about 1962.

Shack's Super Truck Stop was located on U.S. 1, 23, and 301, just south of the Florida-Georgia state line. Typical of the era, the operation is dominated by a large restaurant that catered to both truck and tourist traffic. This photo dates from about 1954.

Pioneer's Rest was an early tourist and truckers' stop along U.S. 66 south of Lincoln, Illinois. In 1937, Ernie Edwards opened his first restaurant in Broadwell, Illinois. Shortly thereafter, a small service station was added next door, originally selling Mobilgas and later Cities Service products. Edwards developed a new type of ham sandwich that he called the "Pig Hip," a specialty that became well known along U.S. 66 in Illinois. Various family members were involved in the enterprise, and Edwards sold his operation to his parents while he was in the military during WWII. The facility was remodeled into its appearance in this 1950 photo during that time. They continued to expand in the postwar boom, and the facility operated until 1991.

The New Jersey turnpike opened in 1952, and each of the service plazas along the road featured Howard Johnson's restaurants and Cities Service gasoline. Again, due to the limited access nature of toll roads, and the food and fuel facilities offered at the service plazas, these served as de facto truck stops, although built primarily to cater to automobile travel. This photo dates from about 1958.

CONOCO and Affiliates

Continental Oil Co.

• Founded in about 1875 in Salt Lake City by Isaac Blake, who had earlier been involved in marketing petroleum in Pennsylvania, and who was also involved in the founding of Pacific Coast Oil in 1879, which eventually became Chevron (Standard Oil Co. of California).

• Continental became affiliated with the Standard Oil Trust in January, 1885. It remained a division of Standard until the 1911 antitrust laws were applied against John D. Rockefeller's oil holdings.

• Merged with Ponca City, Oklahoma's Marland Oil Co. in 1929. Much of what made up CONOCO for most of the twentieth century was rooted in the Marland operations.

• CONOCO was acquired by France's DuPont Corporation in 1981. DuPont offered its shareholders an IPO (Initial Public [stock] Offering) in late 1998, and CONOCO became an independently-held company again in early 1999.

Due to fuel tax differences between states, state line areas are often home to groups of service stations and truck stops. Interstate 65 in southern Indiana is such an area. Cliff's Truck Stop was located just off Interstate 65 at Jeffersonville, Indiana, and was selling CONOCO products when photographed here about 1962.

King's Truck-O-Tel was one of the group of truck stops branded by CONOCO in an expansion in the mid-1960s. Most of the expansion followed the completion of sections of the Interstate Highway System, and this location was on Interstate 40 at Sayre, Oklahoma. Note the irregular roof line and V-form canopies, features typical of 1960s fuel site architecture.

The Cross Roads Truck Stop featured a large enclosed service bay, dorm rooms, and an adjacent restaurant. It was located at the intersection of U.S. 30S, 191 and Utah Route 102, at Tremonton, Utah, and was photographed in 1957.

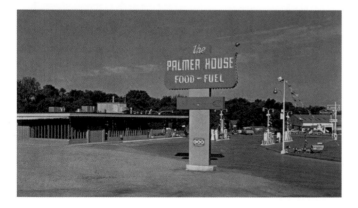

The Palmer House was a restaurant and motel complex on U.S. 20 in Sioux City, Iowa, that also operated as a CONOCO truck stop in the 1950s and 1960s. The motel and restaurant survive today, although fuel sales have long since been discontinued. The facility is shown here as it appeared in the late 1950s.

• CONOCO formed a joint venture with the Flying J truck stop chain on February 01, 1991, and became Flying J's primary supplier of gasoline and diesel fuels.
• Merged with Phillips Petroleum in 2002 to create the third largest integrated oil company in the U.S.—CONOCOPhillips.

Truck Stop Operations

• CONOCO was one of the first gasoline marketers to promote travel, and there were numerous early CONOCO branded outlets that served as de facto truck stops along through routes of the Midwest and Southeast by the middle 1930s.
• No particular attempt was made to organize the existing CONOCO truck stops into a promoted network, as such, but there have been CONOCO branded truck stops from those early pre-WWII efforts to the present.
• In addition to CONOCO branded stops, CONOCO affiliate brands Mileage (Western Oil and Fuel, purchased in 1959) and Kayo (F.P. Kendall Oil, also purchased in 1959) operated truck stops, as well.
• The Mileage operation was rebranded to CONOCO in about 1970, along with their existing truck stops.
• Kayo truck stops (which were company owned and operated) did not appear until the 1980s, about the same time most Kayo stations were rebranded, first to the "Jet" brand, and later to CONOCO.
• *Number of confirmed CONOCO branded truck stops operating in the U.S.:* Fewer than 30 CONOCO

This Colorado scene features two competing truck stops. Wide driveways are a feature of the CONOCO branded facility in the foreground, while a Frontier branded truck stop is seen in the background. This photo dates from about 1958.

Western Oil and Fuel Co. developed a chain of truck stops while still independent, under both its Mileage and DS brands. Later, under CONOCO ownership, the network was enlarged, and locations could then be found throughout Minnesota, Wisconsin, and surrounding states. This location was found on U.S. 53 at Grand Rapids Junction, just west of Duluth, Minnesota. This photo dates from the late 1950s.

branded truck stops have been confirmed (excepting Flying J).

CONOCO Subsidiaries

Kayo (F. P. Kendall & Co.)
• Founded in 1940 by Francis Paul Kendall in Chattanooga, Tennessee, with seven service stations.
• The chain expanded to 40-plus service stations by 1952.
• CONOCO purchased Kendall in 1959. At that time, 171 KAYO branded gas stations were in operation in 11 states.
• CONOCO operated nearly 1,000 KAYO stations as a separate, secondary brand in states throughout the southeastern U.S. until about 1980, when all outlets were rebranded to Jet.
• *Number of confirmed KAYO branded truck stops operating in the U.S.:* No more than seven KAYO branded truck stops can be confirmed, all having operated in the early 1970s.

Western Oil & Fuel
• Founded in 1926 in Minneapolis, Minnesota.
• Originators of the Husky brand and instrumental in the 1938 founding of Cody, Wyoming-based Husky Oil, longtime operator of numerous truck stops.
• Adopted "Mileage" as their primary brand in 1949 after the purchase of the small Duluth, Minnesota, based Zenith Gas that had originated the brand. Would continue to use the Husky name in secondary locations through the late 1950s.

During the 1960s, the Mileage truck stop network was expanded throughout Minnesota and into surrounding states. Shown here is a typical facility, at Pierre, South Dakota.

• In 1956, Western purchased Minneapolis neighbor Direct Service Oil Co. which operated under the DS brand.
• Independently, both Mileage and DS operated truck stops in Minnesota and surrounding states.
• Introduced the Western brand for convenience stores in 1959.
• Purchased by CONOCO in 1959, Western continued as a branded subsidiary through the early 1970s.
• Under CONOCO ownership, the truck stop network in the upper plains states was expanded under the Mileage brand name.

The T and J Truck Stop and Café was located at the edge of the Ozarks, on U.S. 60 at Seneca, Missouri. DX products were sold here, and a complete repair facility and restaurant was located on the premises. This is an excellent example of the typical truck stop of the late 1940s, shown here in about 1950.

DX

Mid Continent Petroleum/Sunray DX

• Mid Continent Petroleum was organized in 1916 in Tulsa, Oklahoma, from the oil holdings of various individuals.

• Began retail marketing of gasoline with the 1920s purchase of Louisville-based Diamond Oil Co. In 1933 Mid Continent introduced a premium grade gasoline named "DX," and by mid-decade, was operating a large network of gas stations in the central U.S. branded "Diamond DX." Stations were rebranded to simply "DX" after WWII.

• Mid Continent merged with Sunray Oil Co. of Tulsa, Oklahoma, in 1955 to become Sunray-Mid Continent Oil Co. The name was revised in 1962 to become DX-Sunray Oil Co.

• DX-Sunray merged with Sun Refining and Marketing Co. (SUNOCO) of Philadelphia, Pennsylvania, in 1968. Shortly thereafter, the SUNOCO brand name replaced DX-Sunray in states where SUNOCO already marketed, specifically Indiana, Illinois, and Kentucky. The DX brand name was retained in other areas in the Midwest, until after 1985 when SUNOCO began to replace DX.

Truck Stop Operations

• *Number of confirmed DX branded truck stops operating in the U.S.:* Nearly a score of DX branded truck stops have been confirmed, all having operated between 1967 and 1984.

EXXON and Affiliates

Standard Oil Company of New Jersey

• Standard Oil Co. of New Jersey was the Standard division that had been assigned marketing in New Jersey, Delaware, Maryland, Virginia, West Virginia, North Carolina, and South Carolina at the 1911 breakup of Standard Oil.

• Operated subsidiary companies Standard Oil Co. of Pennsylvania (Pennsylvania marketing) and Standard Oil Co. of Louisiana, with marketing in Tennessee, Arkansas and Louisiana.

• In 1919, purchased a 50% interest in Humble Oil Company, a Texas producer, refiner and marketer.

• In 1926 introduced ESSO as their premium grade gasoline.

• In 1931, purchased Colonial Beacon Oil Co. and moved into marketing in New England and New York. Colonial Beacon was the product of the 1926 merger of Colonial Oil and Beacon Oil. Colonial Beacon developed very distinctive marketing images and station designs in the 1920s and led the way in marketing automotive products, known as TBA's (tires, batteries, accessories) through their service stations.

• In 1933 ESSO became the company's primary brandname.

• In the 1940s purchased Yale Oil, Grizzly Oil and Powerine Oil in the Rocky Mountain West and began marketing through their Carter Oil subsidiary under the "Oval E" brand. Carter replaced Oval E around 1950.

• In 1956, Standard of New Jersey began a midwestern expansion with the purchase of Milwaukee-based Pate Oil, Indianapolis-based Gaseteria/Bonded, and Chicago private branders Oklahoma Oil and Perfect Power.

• Marketing was consolidated in 1959 under subsidiary Humble Oil Co., which owned and operated the marketing assets of the former ESSO Standard Oil, Humble Oil, Carter Oil, Pate Oil, and Oklahoma Oil companies. Brand names continued as ESSO (east), Humble (Texas), Carter (Rockies and Midwest), Pate (Wisconsin) and Oklahoma (Chicago area).

• In 1960, in an effort at brandname consolidation, Humble introduced the ENCO name to replace Humble, Carter, Pate, and Oklahoma. ESSO remained undisturbed. An expansion in 1961 began the use of the Humble brand in Ohio, after SOHIO objected to both the ESSO and ENCO brands.

In the late 1950s, Standard Oil Co. of New Jersey (ESSO) developed their "Essofleet" brand for independent truck stop operators. For approximately a decade, they experimented with the brand in Virginia and the Carolinas. One independent truck stop operator, F and R Oil Co., opened this facility on U.S. 1 at Ashland, Virginia, in the early 1950s, originally selling Crown products. By the time this 1959 photo was taken the location was selling Essofleet products and featured complete repair facilities and restaurant.

• In 1969 after various courts had rejected use of the ESSO name systemwide, the company began experimenting with brandnames that could be used to replace all three brands. This led to the introduction of EXXON in 1972.

• EXXON merged with Mobil in 1999. Both brands continue in use today. See Mobil section for Mobil history.

Truck Stop Operations

• Prior to the 1950s we are not aware of any efforts by ESSO or any of their affiliates to become involved in any truck stop marketing.

• In the late-1950s ESSO initiated the ESSOFleet brand for a small-scale franchised truck stop operation that would sell ESSO branded products. The venture was relatively short lived, surviving only between about 1959 and 1967, and was never very

This is perhaps the best known travel plaza in the United States. The Pennsylvania Turnpike opened in October of 1940 as the longest (160 miles) four-lane controlled access highway in the U.S. One of the marvels in the development of the highway was the Midway Service Plaza. In these scenes we see the Midway Plaza through more than 25 years of development. During much of its history, including that in these photos, the facility sold ESSO products and operated a Howard Johnson restaurant. Today various chains operate smaller restaurant facilities in the main building, and SUNOCO products are sold at the fuel islands. These early toll road service plazas are a direct forerunner of today's modern travel stops. The two older photos date from the 1940s, the newer one from about 1965.

One of the pioneer truck stops of the Southwest, Tuscon Truck Terminal dates back to at least the late 1940s and originally sold GULF Oil Co. products along U.S. 80. In the early 1960s, the facility changed to the ENCO brand (ESSO's "expansion" brand that was introduced in 1960) and for years made the claim that it was the largest ENCO station. The facility still operates today as part of the Roady's Truck Stop network and it is considered a "must stop" site for truckers and those interested in nostalgia. The photos shown here date from about 1955 (GULF), about 1961 (early ENCO) and from the early 1970s. The brand changed to EXXON in 1973.

widespread.

• ESSOFleet teamed with Southern 500 Truck Stops of Charlotte, North Carolina, on possibly as many as five of their locations in the Carolinas, and at least one location in Virginia.

• As many as a dozen ESSOFleet branded truck stops have been confirmed, all having operated between 1959 and 1968.

• After the introduction of ENCO, various expansions brought the company coast-to-coast marketing. Nearly a dozen ENCO branded truck stops have been confirmed, all having operated between 1962 and 1972.

• EXXON marketers brand numerous regional truck stops today, but EXXON has no official marketing effort to operate truck stops.

EXXON Subsidiaries

Imperial ESSO

• Standard of New Jersey's (later EXXON's) Canadian subsidiary, Imperial Oil markets under the ESSO brand today.

• As many as two dozen Imperial ESSO branded truck stops have been confirmed, all having operated between 1970 and 1995, and all in Canada.

Dallas based American Petrofina (FINA) branded this minimal truck stop on Interstate 30 west of Texarkana, Texas. The facility claims truckers' restaurant, showers, and separate diesel island. It is seen here about 1970.

FINA and Affiliates

American Petrofina

• Founded and owned by Belgium's Petrofina SA.

• Began marketing gasoline in the U.S. in the mid-1950s after having purchased several small independent regional U.S. marketers: Panhandle Oil Co., American Liberty Oil Co. (Amlico), Petro-Atlas Oil Co., and Eldorado Refining Co. (Elreco).

• In the 1963, FINA merged with Cosden Petroleum Co. As far as is known, no truck stops were ever operated under any of the above-listed brands.

• In the late 1960s, American Petrofina purchased the mid-continent operations of TENNECO, and rebranded a number of Bay Oil Co. and TENNECO facilities to FINA, including several truck stops.

• Purchased the marketing properties of Champlin Refining Co. in the mid-1980s, including approximately two dozen branded truck stops and 800 branded gas stations, all of which were rebranded to FINA at that time.

Truck Stop Operations

• *Number of confirmed FINA branded truck stops operating in the U.S.:* Nearly 50 FINA branded truck stops have been confirmed, all having operated between 1970 and 1975.

In the 1940s partners Nathan Segel and Sam Frank founded a truck stop on U.S. 1 in Jersey City, New Jersey, less than two miles from the Holland Tunnel. They settled on the name "Tooley's" for the operation, claiming it had a nice Irish ring to it. They sold Tydol Flying A gasoline and diesel fuel and operated a dorm facility, a restaurant, an extensive truckers' store, and repair facilities. This photo shows the location as it appeared in the early 1950s.

Flying A and its related brands

Tidewater Oil Company, Associated Oil Company, and later Tidewater Associated Oil Co.

• Tidewater Oil Co. was founded in 1887 in New York.

• Associated Oil Co. was founded in 1901 in San Francisco, California, by corporate executives of the Southern Pacific Railroad.

• In 1938, Tidewater and Associated were acquired by J. Paul Getty's Mission Corporation, which defaulted to Standard Oil Co. of New Jersey (ESSO). Under Mission Corporation direction, the companies were merged to form the Tidewater Associated Oil Co. The Mission Corp. also gained control of Skelly Oil Co.

Bishop's Flying A Truck Stop was located on U.S. 101 at the south end of Eureka, California. A large service area offered complete oil changes while truckers dined in the adjoining restaurant. The location is seen here as it appeared about 1960.

The Briar Creek Truck Stop and Restaurant was located on U.S. 11 at Berwick, Pennsylvania, and was selling Flying A products when photographed here about 1962.

Breezewood, Pennsylvania, is one of the most famous highway junctions in the eastern United States, and the area has been home to highway-oriented businesses since the Pennsylvania Turnpike opened in 1940s. One of the businesses operating at Breezewood was the Breezewood Restaurant and Truck Center which, when this photo was taken in about 1960, featured a spacious truck parking lot, and was selling Flying A products.

Tom Walker's Truckers Rendezvous was located at Riverhead, Long Island, New York, and had previously operated (since the 1930s) as Magee's Truck Terminal. In this 1946 photo they were selling Tydol Flying A products and advertising fine food and rooms for truckers.

• After the merger, all eastern U.S. retail sites were branded, "Tydol Flying A," while the western sites remained "Flying A."
• In 1954, nation-wide marketing was consolidated under the Flying A brand, with similar marketing images throughout both the Tydol and Associated territories.
• In the late 1950s, midwestern marketing was sold to Sunray DX.
• In 1966, the West Coast-based former Associated Oil operations of Flying A were sold to Phillips Petroleum, which immediately rebranded every outlet to the Phillips 66 brand.
• In 1970, the Getty brand began to replace the Flying A brand at remaining gas stations in the northeastern U.S. After several changes of ownership, the Getty brand is still in use from Maine to Virginia.

Truck Stop Operations
• *Number of confirmed Flying A branded truck stops operating in the U.S.:*
1958: 34, 24 of which were located in California.
1960: 53, 27 of which were located in California.
1961: 56, 29 of which were located in California.
1962: 57, 32 of which were located in California.
1963: 66, 33 of which were located in California.
1965: 73, 37 of which were located in California.
1966: 69, 33 of which were located in California.
Confirmed truck stop totals drop to approximately a dozen or fewer after the Phillips 66 purchase in 1966. These were located in the remaining East Coast Flying A territory. Presumably, some of these sites survived long enough to be rebranded to the Getty brand in the early 1970s.

Shoop and Schulze Truck Service was one of Associated Oil Co's. earliest truck-oriented service stations. It was located on U.S. Highway 97 in Redmond, Oregon. This 1940s photo is accompanied by an advertisement that indicates that in addition to Associated Flying A gas and diesel fuel, the facility offered dispatching, tire and road service, bunks and showers, and an on-premises restaurant. Shoop and Schulze later became one of the largest tire dealers in the area.

Motor Truck Service opened in January of 1947 as the first modern truck stop on the West Coast. Owners Dick Stricklen and Walter Jaynes came together for this project along convergent paths. Stricklen was the GMC and White Truck dealer for the Bakersfield, California, area while Jaynes had operated Jaynes Garage, which his father had founded in Bakersfield in 1910. During 1944, the two began a partnership, intending to develop a modern super service station. Because wartime restrictions prevented any immediate construction, they traveled through all 48 states analyzing what worked well and what didn't in service station design. The result of the study was a 100,000-square-foot truck stop located on more than 300,000 square feet of paved area; a truck stop that cost more than $750,000 to build and employed more than 200 people. Sixteen pumps in a master-satellite configuration created eight fueling positions, and each island incorporated reels for lube oil, air and water. One photo here shows it shortly after it opened.

Selmer, Tennessee, was home to two early truck stops. Shown here is Thrasher's GULF Truck Stop in a scene from about 1950. Several years after this photo was taken, Pan-Am built a much larger and more modern facility adjacent to this location, and it can be seen elsewhere in this book.

GULF
GULF Oil Corp.

• Founded in Spindletop, Texas, on November 10, 1901 by Anthony Lucas, James Guffey, and John Galey, using money from Pittsburgh's wealthy Mellon family. Originally named the Gulf Refining Company, the enterprise reorganized in 1907 to become The GULF Oil Corporation. At that time a sales office was opened in Atlanta to develop markets in the southeastern U.S.

• GULF built the first designed-for-that-purpose off-street gas station in the world, in Pittsburgh, Pennsylvania, in 1913. It was located at the corner of Baum Blvd. and St. Clair St., and began selling gas on December 1, 1913 for 27 cents per gallon. Within two years, almost every major petroleum marketer had adopted the off-street gas station as a viable alternative to curbside pumps.

• Historians generally agree that the first free road maps were distributed by GULF in Pittsburgh in 1914, although California's Monarch Oil Refining Company may have been distributing them as early as 1911-1912.

• Marketed gasolines and motor oils in nearly 30 southern and eastern states until the 1950s when several purchases of regional gas station chains as well as a large portion of Cities Service's midwestern market-

The Tennessee GULF Truck Stop originally opened as Lampley's in the late 1930s, and incorporated a conventional GULF service station and a restaurant, together in one building. After WWII, diesel fuel was added to the product mix, as were souvenirs and gifts, and the business began to operate as a primitive travel stop. Note the special GULF Diesel Fuel signage, used on stations that were part of GULF's truck stop network of the 1940s and 1950s. Seen here about 1952, it was located on U.S. 31W-41 near Goodlettsville, Tennessee.

ing territory made GULF a coast-to-coast marketer.

• During the late 1950s, GULF operated approximately 39,000 gas stations. The 1970s gas shortages left GULF in serious financial trouble, with their marketing territory shrinking to less than the 30 or so original states, and to less than 22,000 gas stations. After being purchased by Chevron (Standard Oil Co. of California) in 1984, GULF retail marketing was reduced to approximately 15,000 gas stations.

Mitchell's GULF operated as a truck stop on U.S. 80 at Van Horn, Texas. This is an excellent example of how a strategically located gas station that had restaurants and motels nearby could add diesel fuel to their product mix and consider themselves a truck stop. This scene dates from about 1960.

This photo shows typical fuel islands at a GULF branded truck stop that is believed to have been in western Texas. A café can be seen across the street and adjoining the location to the left in this photo. This is an example of a very minimal truck stop location of the late 1940s and early 1950s.

Even as late as the late 1960s, gravel parking lots prevailed at rural truck stops. Rhodes State Line GULF was located on U.S. 67 at Neelyville, Missouri. In addition to truck services and an on-site café, this location also catered to tourists with souvenirs and gifts.

Piedmont Truck Stop/Lemonds Garage is a great example of a 1940s truck stop that survived into the late 1950s. Located on what was then U.S. 29-70, it is coincidentally within a block of where Interstate 40 would eventually cross the highway. The main building featured a trucker-oriented café, while a repair facility was located on an adjacent lot. It is seen here about 1950.

Flynn's Truck Stop was located in Bethune, South Carolina, and was selling GULF products and offering restaurant and sleeping facilities when this photo was shot in about 1962.

• Chevron was forced to sell of certain portions of the GULF marketing. In the southeastern U.S., GULF operations were sold to BP and rebranded to BP in 1990. In the northeastern U.S., GULF operations were sold to Convenience Store operator Cumberland Farms who today operate GULF Oil, LLP.

• GULF operated approximately 4,000 gas stations by the early 1990s.

• In 2010 GULF Oil LLP acquired nationwide rights to the GULF brand. As of this writing, GULF branded gas stations are found all along the eastern seaboard and as far west as Minnesota.

• At least one station in the new expanded marketing area operates as a GULF branded truck stop, located at Galax, Virginia.

Truckstops of America (T/A) originated with two truck stops, one in Rochester, New York, and the other just north of Roanoke at Troutville, Virginia. By the time the chain was incorporated in 1972, four other stops were in operation. All of the original sites sold GULF products.

FAT'S TRUCK STOP
"We Cater to Truckers Exclusively"
South Fork U. S. 15, 15A, 52, Society Hill, S. C.
Phone 2051

Truck Stop Operations
• *Number of confirmed GULF branded truck stops operating in the U.S.:*

Mid-1950s: 617 GULF branded truck stops were listed as operating in the U.S., although most of these locations were simply gas stations that additionally sold diesel fuels, and did not necessarily offer additional services such as truck repair, sleeping facilities, or a restaurant.

1962: 814 GULF branded truck stops were listed as operating in the U.S., although most of these locations were simply gas stations that additionally sold diesel fuels, and did not necessarily offer additional services such as truck repair, sleeping facilities, or a restaurant.

1970: 32
1972: 26
1984: 37

Due to a convergence of highway routes, tiny Society Hill, South Carolina, was home to two major truck stops during the 1950s and 1960s. The older of the two was Fat's, selling GULF products and advertising that it catered exclusively to truckers. In the early 1960s a Southern 500 branded truck stop was located just down the road.

Bigg's Truck Stop is believed to have been in Kentucky. This elaborate building incorporated repair facilities and a café, and was finished in the GULF branding image of the era. This photo dates from about 1950.

Doyal's Truck Stop was located on U.S. 411 at Ranger, Georgia, and is typical of a minimal truck stop of the 1970s. In this instance it appears that a conveniently located GULF service station operation expanded into truck stop status by adding diesel fuel pumps and a restaurant. Most facilities of this type were short-lived in this era.

The 84 Truck Center was another early Gulf branded truck stop in Tucson, Arizona. While some truck stops focus on their driver services (restaurants, bunks, showers, and so forth), the best truck stops offer significant mechanical services as well. At this location, a second photo was necessary in order to show their shop facilities. This photo dates from about 1958.

Many truck stops were located on the outskirts of major cities to appeal to drivers who were "gonna make it through one more town before stopping" or needed to stop for fuel or directions before reaching a major city. Frank's Truck Stop was one such location, positioned on U.S. 52 just north of Winston-Salem, at Rural Hall, North Carolina. This was a very early stop and seems to feature only food and GULF fuels. This photo dates from the late 1940s.

Often truck dealers would find themselves in the position of operating a de facto truck stop. One example of this was the GMC dealership in Essington, Pennsylvania. While many car dealerships were also elaborate gas stations, this GMC truck agency made the logical step of adding GULF diesel fuel in an era when diesel fuel was still a rarity. Some dealerships like this evolved into full-fledged truck stops, some into larger dealerships, and unfortunately, some into oblivion. This photo dates from about 1948.

Jeff's Truck Stop was a small fuel and food type stop located in Kadoka, South Dakota. Frontier Oil Co. products were being sold here when photographed in 1962.

HUSKY and Affiliates

HUSKY Oil Co.

• Western Oil & Fuel Co., founded in 1926 in Minneapolis, Minnesota, was the creator of the Husky brand. Western operated Husky branded outlets until the late 1950s.

• The Husky Oil Co. was set up in Cody, Wyoming in 1938, under partial ownership of Western Oil.

• In the late-1940s, Husky began Canadian operations, opening a refinery in Lloydminster, Alberta.

• In 1954, Husky's U.S. operations merged with H. Earl Clack, Inc., a chain of service stations located in Montana, Wyoming, and surrounding regions, and brought the Husky brand to the northern Rocky Mountain region through Clack. Clack had been operating these gas stations and truck stops under their HECCO brand name until all operations were consolidated under the Husky brand after Western's purchase.

• In 1960, the U.S. Husky operations came under control of the formerly independent Canadian-based Husky Oil.

• In 1967, Husky Oil purchased Denver-based Frontier Oil Co., a gasoline marketer in the Rocky Mountain West.

• Nearly 500 North American Husky branded outlets were in operation by 1980.

• In 1984, the entire U.S. Husky Oil operation was sold to Flying J. However, only 24 of the U.S. truck stops and 12 of the service stations were at that point Husky-owned. The remaining Husky branded outlets were owned by independent distributors.

• Husky's truck stop chain was second in size only to UNION 76 (later UNOCAL) in the western U.S. at the time of the Flying J acquisition, with locations in 13 western states, and in western Canadian provinces.

Truck Stop Operations

• *Number of confirmed Husky branded truck stops operating in the U.S.:*

• Two Husky Oil predecessor companies were heavily involved in truck stop operations before their affiliation with Husky. H. Earl Clack was operating primitive truck stops and tourist facilities as far back as the 1930s, and Frontier Oil Co. operated an extensive network of truck stops throughout their marketing territory. Both company's former management personnel were instrumental in Husky's truck stop operations.

• As many as 66 Husky branded truck stops can be confirmed as operating in the U.S. between 1970 and the purchase of the Husky brand by Flying J in 1984.

• As many as 36 Husky truck stops have reportedly operated in Canada from Bradford, Ontario to Prince George, British Columbia.

Gasoline marketer H. Earl Clack was an early promoter of tourism in the northern Rocky Mountain area. Several of Clack's early "Hi Power" stations were forerunners of today's travel plazas. After the Husky Oil Co. purchased Clack's operation in 1954, Husky began development of a full-scale truck stop program. The Lee Lewis Super Stop was one of the early Husky truck stops. Located on U.S. 2 in Kalispell, Montana, this stop featured a large truck repair facility along with the usual food and fuel. It is seen here as it appeared in the late 1950s.

In 1950, Joe Johnson began construction on a new truck stop to be located on U.S. 87 in a rural location 43 miles north of Denver, Colorado. It would be known as "Johnson's Corner." Frontier brand gasoline and diesel fuel sales were supplemented by a café and a truck repair facility. Over the years, additional Johnson-operated locations were added to this small network, and for a while, fuel was private-branded under the Johnson's name. Today, Johnson's Corner continues to be known as one of the "must stop" truck stops of the Rockies. The older of these two photos dates from about 1958, the latter from 1965.

McGaffick's is an example of how a strategically located service station, which represented a brand known for its early truck stop network, could take conventional facilties and operate them in a manner such that they evolve into a truck stop. A large "Diesel" sign seems to be the only feature that allows the owner to describe this station as a truck stop. In reality, a small café is also located on the property; the service bays are large enough to accommodate trucks. Located at the intersection of U.S. 10 and U.S. 91 in Helena, Montana, this photo dates from about 1958.

In addition to the U.S. 87 location, Johnson's Corner operated another truck stop, this one on U.S. 85 at Sedalia, Colorado. Smaller than the original, Frontier brand fuels were sold here, as well. This photo dates from about 1957.

Another early Husky truck stop is the Bud Lake Super Stop, located on U.S. 10 and U.S. 93 in Missoula, Montana. This facility includes a larger-than-most café, a tire dealership, and an International Harvester truck dealership. It was photographed in about 1962.

Green River, Wyoming, was home to this Husky branded truck stop and café, shown here in about 1964.

In the sparsely populated Rocky Mountain states, many service stations in the mid-twentieth century essentially became truck stops, simply because stations in this area were so few and far between. Frontier Refining, as a marketer in this area, operated or branded a disproportionate number of truck stops for the size of the company. This location, at East Limon, Colorado, is an example of one such stop. Simply selling Frontier diesel fuel and operating a café allowed a dealer to call his station a truck stop. This facility is as it appeared in about 1954.

FRONTIER SERVICE & CAFE
"Truck Stop"
East Limon, Colorado
Highways 287~40~24~71
Always Open
All Credit Cards Accepted

In the 1960s, many of the somewhat primitive truck stops of earlier years gave way to more modern, more complete facilities; in effect, a transition from Second Generation truck stops to Third Generation. Frontier facilities were updated as part of this general trend. This location, John's Truck Stop, was located on U.S. 91 in Fillmore, Utah, and contrasts greatly with the earlier Frontier food and fuel facility in East Limon, Colorado, that is seen elsewhere in this book. This photo dates from about 1964.

Williams Husky Truck Stop, shown in the 1970s after most of the Frontier network had converted to Husky. Located at Interstate 80 and Hershey Road in Hershey, Nebraska.

This unknown location is an example of where a service station operator saw an opportunity when a large amount of truck traffic began passing his station, and added diesel fuel to the product mix in an effort to increase sales. This photo shows the oldest example where Deep Rock brand diesel fuel was offered. Whether location or product, the truck traffic seen here shows that the effort brought results in this late 1930s photo.

Kerr McGee and Deep Rock

Kerr McGee Oil Industries and Deep Rock Oil Corp.

• Deep Rock was founded in Cushing, Oklahoma, in about 1913.

• Purchased by Kerr McGee in 1955. At that time, Deep Rock was operating more than 1,000 gas stations in 16 midwestern states.

• By 1960, Deep Rock was operating in 17 states from Minnesota to New Mexico, and east as far as Mississippi.

• Kerr McGee's Deep Rock operations were 100% jobber controlled. Although the Deep Rock name was phased out in favor of the Kerr McGee brand in the 1980s, some Deep Rock branded sites are known to have existed until as late as 1995.

Truck Stop Operations

• *Number of confirmed Deep Rock branded truck stops operating in the U.S.:* Only a handful of Deep Rock branded truck stops have been confirmed, all having operated between 1960 and 1979.

Although the signage would lead one to believe that this facility is more of a travel stop than a truck stop, make no mistake about the range of services offered here. The facility included a 60-foot lube and wash bay, bunk rooms, driver lounge and TV room, driver dispatch service, and more. This stop was operated by Wylie Petroleum Co., the local jobber selling Kerr McGee's Deep Rock products. It was located on U.S. 70 in Floydada, Texas, and is seen here in about 1965.

Rollette Oil Co., the Kerr McGee Deep Rock jobber in Beloit, Wisconsin, operated this truck stop on Milwaukee Rd. for many years. It is shown here with both the then-current Kerr McGee, and the dated Deep Rock dual branding when photographed in 1990.

Marathon and Affiliates

Marathon Oil Co.

• Founded on August 1, 1887, as the Ohio Oil Co. Standard purchased the company in 1889.

• Assigned oil production and exploration with the 1911 breakup of the Standard Oil Co.

• Purchased Robinson, Illinois-based Lincoln Oil Co. to enter gasoline marketing, using Lincoln Oil's Linco brand.

• Purchased Pittsburgh, Pennsylvania-based Transcontinental Oil and their Marathon brand in 1930. At that time, Transcontinental marketed from Texas and Oklahoma east to the Carolinas and Georgia.

• Marketed petroleum products under both the Linco and Marathon names until 1939, when the Linco name was phased out and Marathon became the surviving brand. Widespread marketing was abandoned during WWII in favor of focused marketing in Illinois, Indiana, Ohio, and portions of Michigan and Kentucky.

• Purchased Detroit-based Speedway Petroleum in 1959. The Speedway 79 brand was phased out in favor of the Marathon brand name, beginning in 1962.

• The corporate name was changed to Marathon Oil in 1962.

• In 1962, Marathon Oil purchased Plymouth Oil Co. Plymouth Oil was the successor to Republic Oil Co., and Plymouth continued to market under the Republic brand name. Marathon made the purchase to gain access to Plymouth's extensive unbranded marketing in the southern U.S., but retained use of the Republic brand during a slow-paced phase out that lasted approximately 20 years.

• During the 1960s Marathon branded outlets operated in Ohio, Illinois, Indiana, Michigan, Kentucky, then later along I-75 in Tennessee, Georgia, and Florida.

• Beginning in 1972, Marathon Oil began purchasing various marketing companies that operated in their general area. Most of these operations were employee-operated chains. Marathon would cultivate an extensive direct retail operation based on their experiences with these chains. Eventually this operation would become Emro Marketing (Emro for Marathon Retail Operations) and would adopt a reintroduced Speedway brand.

• In the 1990s Speedway would develop an extensive truck stop network, with locations throughout much of the eastern U.S.

• In a joint venture with the Ashland Oil Co., Marathon Ashland Petroleum Co. was formed to operate the branded marketing controlled by both Marathon and Ashland. This merger led to the merger of Marathon's and Ashland's direct retail operations to form Speedway SuperAmerica LLC. SuperAmerica's truck stop network was rebranded to the Speedway brand name at this time.

Truck Stop Operations

• *Number of confirmed Marathon branded truck stops operating in the U.S.:* A total of 12 Marathon branded truck stops can be confirmed, all having operated between 1971 and 1995.

• Today, Marathon's jobber network operates several dozen truck stops.

Marathon Subsidiaries

• Marathon's Emro Marketing consisted of the directly-operated gas station chains that Marathon began purchasing in 1972. These brands included Consolidated, Bonded, Gastown, Value, Globe/Starvin-Marvin, Ecol, Cheker, Port, and various Rock Island-owned brands. Martin Oil Co. and Wake Up Oil Co. were added after the consolidation to the Speedway brand had begun in the late-1980s. Several of these subsidiary brands were involved in truck stop operations. During the conversion to the Speedway brand name, Speedway achieved prominence as a significant U.S. truck stop operator.

• In 2001, the Speedway truck stop network was sold to Pilot Oil Co. Pilot's history with Marathon had included a stint wherein they had been a partially-owned subsidiary. It was the merger of Speedway into Pilot that brought Pilot to its present status as one of the largest truck stop operators in the U.S.

Art Hague's Truck Center was located on Interstate 10 in Tucson, Arizona. It was comprised of a Cummins Diesel service facility and a Mobil-gas branded truck stop. A large canopy structure covered most of the fuel center, and it was topped by a large Mobil sign that was a variation of the design introduced in 1955. A small café located adjacent to the service facility completed the layout for this classic truck stop.

Mobil and Affiliates

Standard Oil Co. of New York, and Vacuum Oil Co., later SOCONY-Vacuum Oil Co., still later SOCONY-Mobil Oil Co.

• The Standard Oil Co. of New York (SOCONY) was founded in 1882. SOCONY began retail marketing of gasolines in New York and New England in about 1915. Was marketing coast-to-coast by about 1930, having purchased Magnolia Petroleum, General Petroleum, and White Eagle Oil and Refining Co.

• Vacuum Oil Co. was founded in 1866 and was also a Standard Oil subsidiary. After the breakup of Standard Oil in 1911, Vacuum Oil Co, originators of the Mobiloil trademark, merged with Lubrite Refining Co., Wadhams Oil Co., and White Star Refining Co. in an effort to become an integrated operation.

• SOCONY and Vacuum merged in 1931, adopting an image that included SOCONY's flying red horse and Vacuum's "Mobilgas" brand. The Mobilgas

The Triangle Truckport was an oil company adaptation to a First Generation type truck stop. Founded by Harlan Hagburg in 1953, the Triangle Truckport was located at the intersection of U.S. 6 and U.S. 350, just north of Davenport, Iowa. The location was rebranded to PURE by 1957 as PURE's truck stop program expanded across the country. In 1962, Interstate 80 bypassed the location and the business was refocused to become a family restaurant. It remains in operation today. This photo dates from 1956.

Mobil jobber Jess Taylor saw the opportunity that the new Interstate highway system presented, and in 1963 began construction on the Interstate Service Truck Stop on U.S. 77 at Interstate 90 in Sioux Falls, South Dakota. More than $600,000 was invested in the 21 pump fueling facility, which also included 42,000 gallons of storage capacity. The large restaurant, known as the Truck Haven Café, was incorporated into a single building complex that included a conventional Mobil station of the era, supplemented by an extra service bay for trucks. Bunk rooms upstairs completed the operation. A similar facility was built during 1964 off Interstate 29 in N. Sioux City, Iowa. This photo shows the Sioux Falls facility as it appeared in the late 1960s.

brand name was phased-in through the various subsidiary marketing operations during the 1930s.

• After a considerable period of expansion through the 1930s, '40s, and '50s, the company was re-named Mobil Oil Corp. in 1966.

• Historically, Mobilgas was marketed nationwide, except in the southern U.S. Expansion into this area began in the 1940s and by the 1970s, Mobil stations could be found in most states. After the gas shortages of the 1970s, Mobil began selling or closing large portions of its marketing operations.

• Mobil Oil merged with EXXON in 1999 and today the company operates as EXXONMobil. Marketing remains strong in some of the historically significant Mobil marketing areas, particularly in the northeastern and upper Midwest regions, and in Florida. The Mobil brand is also offered to EXXON jobbers as a secondary brand.

Truck Stop Operations

• *Number of confirmed Mobil branded truck stops operating in the U.S.:* Mid-late 1960s: 456 Mobil branded truck stops were listed as operating in the U.S., although most of these locations were simply gas stations that additionally sold diesel fuels, and did not necessarily offer additional services such as truck repair, sleeping facilities, or a restaurant. Of these 456, 49 can be confirmed as Mobil branded truck stops.

• Approximately 30 Mobil branded truck stops can be confirmed as having operated between 1970 and 1985.

Phillips Petroleum

• Company was founded by Frank Phillips in Bartlesville, Oklahoma, in 1917.

• Began retail marketing of gasoline on November 19, 1927 from a single gas station located in Wichita, Kansas. Additional gas stations were opened several weeks later in Salina and Topeka, Kansas, as well as in Bartlesville.

• Rapid expansion through aggressive gas station construction, as well as acquisition of smaller competing companies resulted in a network of more than 12,000 gas stations by the end of WWII.

• Purchased Tidewater Associated's West Coast gas stations in 1966, then opened a single gas station in

Bill Lepard operated the Lepard 66 Truck Station on U.S. 180 at Anson, Texas. This classic truck stop included eleven pumps for Phillips gasoline and diesel fuels, and butane storage and dispensing for refrigeration equipment. Despite promotion as a truck stop, this facility does not appear to include a restaurant, although there were probably diners nearby. This photo dates from about 1957.

Landmark Truck Stop and Restaurant is a great example of 1960s Third Generation truck stop design. Service station, restaurant, and repair facilities were housed in a large central building, with gas islands in front and multiple diesel islands to the side. Pumps were fed from large above-ground storage tanks. Imitation wood paneling covered the vertical surfaces in the restaurant, which included a truckers-only lunch counter and tables for any patron. Landmark was located on Interstate 80 at Odessa Rd., Odessa, Nebraska, and was photographed here in about 1968.

Anchorage, Alaska, in 1967, making Phillips only the second oil company to market retail petroleum products in all 50 states, behind TEXACO (with branded truck stops operating in only the lower 48 states).
• Began abandoning its widespread marketing during the 1970s gas shortages, first in the northeast and on the West Coast, then later in the southeastern U.S.
• Phillips 66 merged with CONOCO in 2002 to become CONOCO/Phillips.

Truck Stop Operations

Number of confirmed Phillips 66 branded truck stops operating in the U.S.:
• As many as 585 truck stops are confirmed as having been operated by Phillips Petroleum Co. as of 1970; likely many of these were retail gas stations that also operated a diesel pump.
• NTS confirms 86 Phillips branded truck stops operating as of 1970, with as many as 102 operating as of 1975.
• Phillips branded jobbers continue to operate some truck stop sites under the Phillips 66 brand today.

A former truck driver, Les Fuller, developed this minimal fuel stop on U.S. 80 in Colorado City, Texas, in the early 1950s. It appears that the bunkroom and shower facilities were upstairs in the main building, with a café on an adjacent lot. Note the specialty Phillips shield sign listing discounts offered on fuel pricing to truckers. Shown here in about 1953, this facility was rebranded and added to the Skelly Oil Co. truck stop network in the early 1960s.

You can almost hear Dave Dudley singing in the background when looking at this photo. Truck City was located on U.S. 31W-41 six miles north of Nashville, Tennessee, and was the site of the photo shoot for the album cover for the original release of the song, "Six Days On The Road." A small bunkhouse was located behind the fuel desk area. It is seen here in about 1964, when Phillips 66 products were being sold.

Pete and Sons Place was a locally-developed Phillips 66 branded truck stop on U.S. 60-66 in Amarillo, Texas. This facility, too, takes a very minimal approach to truck stop design. It was photographed about 1956.

Leu's Truck Stop was an example of a Second Generation truck stop with facilities located in separate buildings. While this photo shows a minimal fuel and service area, albeit with an elaborate pylon sign with neon Phillips 66 shield and lettering, a café and bunkhouse existed elsewhere on the property. Shown here about 1957, Leu's was located on the U.S. 80-85 truck route around Las Cruces, New Mexico.

The Wheel Stop, located on U.S. 231 in Jasper, Indiana, is an interesting facility. Repair bays were located in the center of the building, with service station fuel desk located on one side and a small "short order" restaurant on the other side. This photo of this compact truck stop dates from about 1954.

Truck Arena was located on U.S. 16 east of Chamberlain, South Dakota, and consisted of a restaurant grafted onto the rear of an otherwise relatively conventional Phillips 66 gas station of the era. Repair bays were located on the back of the building, out of sight in this photo, which is from about 1957.

Servicetown was a forward-looking concept developed by North Carolina businessman, politician, and philanthropist Frank Kenan. Kenan started in the oil business as the PURE Oil Co. commission agent in Durham, North Carolina. After learning the disadvantages of operating as a commission agent, he set up Kenan Oil as a distributorship. In addition to building his distributorship into one of North Carolina's most successful, Kenan founded Kenan Transport Co. in 1943, building it into one of the nation's largest fuel transport operations. He also founded Tops Petroleum Co. in 1947, operating a discount chain of stations in competition with major brand stations, including his own. In the early 1950s, Kenan Oil became one of the first Phillips jobbers in North Carolina, and helped to establish the brand in the growing Triangle area. Phillips Petroleum backed Kenan on the development of his Servicetown truck stops, the first of which opened in Durham in the early 1960s. Another Servicetown opened in Fredricksburg, Virginia, in 1966, and still another in Greenville, South Carolina, in the same era. This photo shows the Durham location at about the time it opened. The complex included a branch of the Honey's Restaurant operation, a Charlotte based chain. Today, all that remains is Honey's Restaurant, as the rest of the site has been redeveloped for retail use.

Developed from a small roadside service station, the Florianna Truck Stop was a rare late example of adapting an early gas station for truck stop use. Phillips 66 products were being sold here when photographed in the early 1960s. The Florianna was located in Fort Ogden, Florida.

The Big Spring Truck Terminal was a large truck stop facility located near U.S. 80 in Big Spring, Texas. Included in the central structure was a fuel facility and truckers' store, the "66 Café," a large service area and wash bay, along with the requisite upstairs bunkhouse. Phillips 66 products were sold here when this photograph was taken in 1958.

When Phillips Petroleum began marketing in Florida in 1953, a massive effort was made to build up the brand in the state. Jobbers that signed with Phillips were encouraged to build non-conventional stations, including marinas, airport locations, and truck stops. The Oasis Truck Stop, on U.S. 441 in Fort Lauderdale, Florida, was built during this big Phillips expansion. The Oasis advertised that all of their parking was paved, and that they offered extensive service facilities, including on-site scales, individual sleeping rooms, TV lounge and reading room, and a truckers' store and restaurant. The Oasis is seen here in about 1962.

Built in the configuration of the conventional Phillips 66 stations of the 1960s, the oversized service bays are the only real indication that truck-related business was solicited, and this location, The Oasis 66 Truck Stop, promoted itself as seeking truck-related business. The Happy Chef restaurant in the background of the photo rounded out the offering to truckers. Located on U.S. 169 in North Mankato, Minnesota, it is likely that this location reverted to conventional service station status within a few years after this shot was taken. It is seen here in about 1964.

This fuel island photo shows two Kenworth cabovers fueling at a Phillips 66 fuel island somewhere in the Midwest. The photo dates from the early 1960s.

PURE Oil Co. and Affiliates

The PURE Oil Co., USA

• The company that we today know as the PURE OIL Co. has its roots in petroleum exploration activities around Oil City, Pennsylvania, in the early 1890s. The major predecessors were later organized as the Producers Oil Co.

• In 1895, Producers Oil and various other interests came under control of a New Jersey holding company known as the Pure Oil Company. This was the first use of the Pure Oil name.

• Ohio Cities Gas Co. was organized as a public utility holding company in 1914, owning and operating a number of natural gas facilities in various Ohio municipalities. Exploration for gas reserves led to the discovery of crude oil in West Virginia in December 1914, thus placing Ohio Cities in the oil business.

• The Ohio Cities Gas Co. purchased the Pure Oil Company in 1917. Placing more emphasis on its petroleum business interests, Ohio Cities was renamed The PURE Oil Company in 1920. From this point the Dawes family, majority owners of PURE, began to sell their municipal gas systems interests in order to concentrate exclusively on their oil and gasoline interests. Disregarding their earlier history, PURE would choose the 1914 organization of Ohio Cities Gas as its point of origin.

• In 1921, a separate Pure Oil Company, this one based in Minnesota, was purchased by PURE Oil. Other 1920s acquisitions include Sherrill Oil (Pensacola, Florida), Wofford Oil Company (Atlanta, Georgia and Birmingham, Alabama), Seaboard Oil (Jacksonville, Florida), American Oil (Hattiesburg, Mississippi), and Colonial Oil (Norfolk, Virginia).

• In 1927, PURE introduced a "Cottage Style" gas station designed to blend in to residential neighborhoods. Architectural features included steeply-pitched roofs, one (sometimes twin) chimneys, a bay window with planter boxes beneath, a rounded-arch doorway on the main entrance, and extensive residential-style landscaping. The first one was constructed in Indianapolis. Many of these cottage style stations were modified and expanded, and served as truck stops well into the mid-late 1960s.

• In 1928, PURE acquired a controlling interest in Toledo, Ohio-based Hickok Oil Co. This purchase, one of many in the 1920s, would be instrumental in PURE's rise in truck stop marketing in the 1950s.

• By 1938, PURE had expanded its marketing terri-

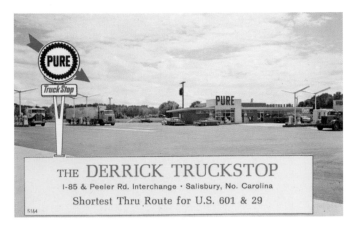

The Derrick Truck Stop (PURE Truck Stop #247) first shows up in the 1962 PURE Truck Directory, but only as a planned construction. The 1963 edition displays a pre-Grand Opening photo. This shot is from about 1965. At this time, Wade Weddle was the operator. "10 acres of parking" was one of The Derrick's main draws for truckers, as well as it being located on I-85 at the Peeler Rd. Interchange, which was touted as being the "shortest thru route for U.S. 601 & 29." At left is a White Freightliner cabover, and an International Emeryville cabover; at center, a 1962 Ford Galaxie is visible, while a White conventional sits at the fuel islands at right.

Speed & Briscoe (PURE Truck Stop #210) was one of the more famous truck stops on the East Coast during the '60s, noted mostly for its modern facilities and aggressive advertising. This early Third Generation truck stop was located in Ashland, Virginia, and was operated by Lee Speed and "Bris" Briscoe. It was located on U.S. Highway 1, which at the time, was the "main" thoroughfare linking Maine to Florida. This shot dates from the late 1950s, shortly after construction.

tory through multiple acquisitions, and was supplying nearly 17,000 PURE branded outlets with petroleum products.

• PURE purchased the remaining portion of the Hickok Oil Co. in about 1951, adding approximately 1,600 additional retail outlets. In 1935, Hickok had originated the truck stop concept at a single location in Imlay City, Michigan; a concept that PURE later expanded into a network of nearly 350 truck stops by the late 1960s.

AMBER TRUCK STOP
U.S. #1 & #78
NORTH AUGUSTA, SOUTH CAROLINA

The Great Northern Auto-Truck Service PURE Truck Stop (#405) dates from 1958. At that time, H. D. "Mike" Michelsen operated this new construction, located at the intersection of U.S. Highway 112 and M-56 (45475 Michigan Ave). in Belleville, Michigan. This particular layout employs the abstracted PURE cube (first used in nearby Imlay City by the Hi-Speed Oil Co. on the world's first truck stop) as the entrance to the diesel truck service garage. Upstairs sleeping facilities are behind.

One mile northeast of Augusta, Georgia, in North Augusta, South Carolina, The Amber Truck Stop (#628), operated by Glenn E. Fox, was sited on the east side of U.S. Highway 1, and dates to the late 1950s as a PURE branded outlet. It appears to have been built in the early 1950s as an AMOCO-designed facility. In addition to the smattering of carefree puffy white summertime clouds, these photos of The Amber are a visual cornucopia: Triangular amber-colored neon "Amber Truck Stop" signage sits atop a glass brick-faced central pylon; a restaurant advertises, "Thick Shakes," "Bar-B-Q," and "Ranch Burgers" at roofline; and a newly-constructed motel sits behind. By 1960, the "Amber" signage atop the pylon had vanished, and the original main building had been extended to the right to now include an "Air Conditioned Drivers' Lounge" with TV. By 1963, Joe Goodgame was in charge, and continued to steward the Amber through the rebranding to a UNION 76 outlet. By then, even the restaurant had been enlarged.

• PURE was purchased by the Union Oil Co. of California in 1965. In 1968, Union 76 began rebranding all PURE outlets to the 76 brand. The rebranding process was termed "complete" by 1970 and PURE "officially" ceased to exist.

• In 1993, the PURE brand was resurrected by the Southeastern Oil Jobbers Cooperative, who continue to expand the brand's retail gasoline marketing area today; at least one PURE Oil jobber, Horn Oil Company of Mocksville, North Carolina, operates a truck stop today that is branded PURE.

• *Number of confirmed PURE branded truck stops operating in the U.S. by year:*

1957: 168
1958: 174
1960: 234
1961: 256
1962: 252
1963: 273
1965: 282
1966: 278
1967: 337
1969: 295
Early 1970s: 289

Operator Charles Allen's Charleston-Huntington PURE Truck Plaza (#198) first appeared in the PURE Truck Stop Directories in the late 1960s, although this shot was likely taken earlier, judging by the 1962 Chevrolet Corvair and the 1964 Ford Galaxie facing the camera. Located at I-64 and State Route 34 approximately midway between Huntington and Charleston, West Virginia, this Third Generation truck stop perhaps started life branded as an oil company other than PURE, as there is no abstracted PURE pylon/cube nor corresponding PURE neon blue lettering atop the building.

PURE's 1966 Truck Stop Directory shows Wapakoneta, Ohio's Wapak Truck Plaza (PURE Truck Stop #149) from an angle roughly opposite from that in the 1960 Directory. Robert Richardson is now listed as the proprietor. A large plastic backlit PURE Truck Stop sign has been added above the second story "showers and roomettes" building sometime since 1960. The additional services added since 1960 include: weight scales, clothing, liquid propane, a TV lounge, a barber shop, and block and blown ice. The lot still appears to be of graveled-dirt. At left can be seen a (left to right): a B-61 Mack conventional, an International, a GMC COE, and a 1950s-era 660-series Diamond T conventional tractor.

The "Windmill Pure Oil TruckStop" (#355) dates as a PURE outlet from 1961. Originally located in Diamondale, Michigan, at that time, by the time the 1962 PURE Truck Stop Directory was published, it was "relocated" to Lansing, although it physically had not moved from its U.S. Highway 27 roadside. Early photos suggest that this was a Second Generation Mom & Pop operation (a farmhouse is located to the right of the gas station photo). C. V. Aikin managed this tidy operation until at least the early 1970s, by which time Don Millisor (the "Don" of Don's Restaurant?) was listed as operator.

The Trail Service Center (PURE Truck Stop #631), operated by Jessee W. Tucker in this pre-1960 photo, was located on U.S. Highway 301, four miles east of Tampa, Florida. To the left are likely the sleeping facilities, with the eatery at right. By the time the 1962 PURE Truck Stop Directory was published, this outlet was no longer listed.

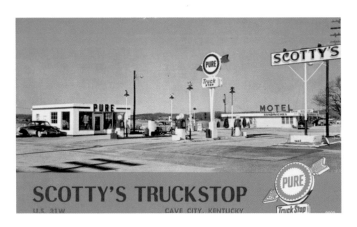

Located on U.S. Highway 31W in Cave City, Kentucky, "Scotty," whomever he was, certainly operated a clean, attractive, inviting, truck stop PURE Truck Stop (#330). The fuel building showcases several oil can pyramids in the windows; the large neon MOTEL signage sits atop a cornice that also advertises Sandwiches and Barbecue (and additionally features a neon EAT sign); behind that, and barely visible, is more neon advertising a DAIRY BIG DIP dairy bar (frozen custard, anyone…?) Three fuel islands featuring four globe-topped fuel pumps, and two pumps of the newer 1960s variety sit on concrete pads surrounded by dusty asphalt. A '52 Buick rests at left.

An artist's rendering in the 1965 PURE Truck Stop Directory becomes the Effingham PURE Truck Plaza (#379) by 1966. Jim McDaniels was the first operator of this outlet, located at the intersection of I-70 and I-57, and was still in charge by the time of the 1970 PURE rebranding to UNION 76. This Third Generation's teardrop-shaped paved lot is augmented by a graveled parking area behind the twin service bays, while autos are allowed parking at the front of the building and are also allowed to nose-up to the restaurant, following the Third Generation dictum of the separation of truck and auto traffic.

The artist's rendering of Frank Talarico's State Line Service Center, Inc. (#159) in 1960 differs considerably from the actual construction shown here in 1961, mainly in its placement of signage and its idealized elaborateness. It was located at U.S. Highway 6 and the Erie Thruway (I-90). Oddly, what was billed as "The World's Finest Truck Stop" in 1961 fails to be listed in the 1966 PURE Truck Stop Directory, or beyond.

Is this a slightly later incarnation of Scotty's Truck Stop in Cave City, Kentucky (#330), or a different PURE Truck Stop in the same town? Both are located on U.S. Highway 31W, in Cave City. Having been shot from a different angle, there are few revealing clues here. Even the angle of the red neon arrow on the PURE Truck Stop sign is a bit different. It would seem unlikely that there would be two competing PURE Truck Stops, both on the same road, in a small town such as Cave City…

Robin Hood Pure TruckStop

INTERSTATE 95 .... BENSON, NORTH CAROLINA

In 1957, the "Robin Hood PURE TruckStop" (#243) was located between Dunn and Benson, North Carolina, at the intersection of I-95 and Denning Rd. Sometime prior to 1963, Whitley Hood began his stewardship of this establishment. The facility would make the transition to UNION 76 in 1970 and remain in operation as a UNION 76 truck stop into the 1990s.

SUPER SERVICE STATION

U.S. 421 & ROUTES 115 & 268   North Wilkesboro, North Carolina

Dating from the late 1950s as a PURE branded outlet, North Wilkesboro's Super Service Station (#209) was located at 200 B St., at the intersection of several through routes. H. Baker was the operator at the time that this photo was taken; Paul Cashion assumed control in 1965, and was replaced by Bill Dawson by the time of the UNION 76 takeover of PURE. A Coke button-bedecked diner is at left, with a two-bay diesel service garage and fuel island office at center. Sleeping facilities are listed in various PURE Truck Stop Directories, but are apparently not visible here. A late 1950s Dodge wrecker (#990) can be seen at far right.

CARTER TRUCK TERMINAL

U.S. No. 441, 17, 92—3¾ MILES NORTH OF ORLANDO, FLORIDA

PURE CITY TRUCKSTOP

Routes (S441-17-92) . . . 5425 S. Orange Blossom Trail
ORLANDO, FLORIDA

The PURE City Truck Stop, also in Orlando, Florida, at 5425 S. Orange Blossom Trail (PURE Truck Stop #652), had been known as Harold Carter's "Carter Truck Terminal" until it became Walter E. Smith's establishment after a remodeling in about 1962. At that time, a battery of motel rooms, a barber shop, teletype services, icing facilities, a drivers' lounge, a post office, Western Union services, and a laundromat/dry cleaner service had all been added. This shot shows a late 1950s International conventional fueling at the newly-expanded diesel islands, at left. A DeSoto auto can be seen nosed up to the restaurant, at right.

U.S. 250 and 36, **AL'S** TruckStop
3 Miles East DENNISON, OHIO

Al Pica's "Al's Truck Stop" (#128) was under construction in 1958, and fully operational by 1959. Located three miles east of Dennison, Ohio, on U.S. Highways 250 and 36, this Third Generation truck stop displays the all-under-one-roof-type of construction that was beginning to become the hallmark of the genre. However, one foot remains in the past with the graveled parking area. A late 1950s GMC DR-860 and an early 1950s Diamond T can bee seen at right, in the gravel. Sam Ruefly took over the reins at this station in 1963, and re-named it the S & E PURE Plaza. He and the name remained until the PURE conversion to UNION 76 occurred in 1970.

This tidy little truck stop is a visual delight. Orlando, Florida's Carter Truck Terminal, located at the intersection of U.S. Highways 441, 17, and 92 (4949 N. Orange Blossom Trail), prominently displays its Thermo-King Refrigeration Sales and Service facilities via two signs facing the roadway at a 90-degree angle. Five fuel pumps sit on a concrete pad surrounded by a graveled-dirt approach. It appears as though the café is at left, behind the pumps, with dorm facilities located on the second floor, and also perhaps near center, beneath the neon Thermo-King signage (note the twin screen doors below the signage, and the picnic table-type bench between). The truck stop's spiffy early-1950s PURE blue-and-white GMC pickup proudly poses at the corner of the building; a late-50s cabover Mack exits the service facility.

Ohio 71-35 TruckStop

Interstate 71 and U.S. 35   •   Jeffersonville, Ohio

Joseph M. Garner's Ohio 71-35 Truck Stop (#187) was constructed in about 1965 at the intersection of U.S. Highways 71 and 35, in Jeffersonville, Ohio. This aerial shot shows the expansive parking, fuel islands at right, and a curious "loop" road-to-nowhere behind the lot.

CAPITAL CITY TRUCKSTOP

U.S. #1—10 MILES NORTH, RALEIGH, NORTH CAROLINA

Wayne F. Gibson's Capital City Truck Stop (PURE Truck Stop #238) was located 10 miles north of Raleigh, North Carolina, on U.S. Highway 1. Constructed in about 1961, the sandy white North Carolina soil coupled with the pure white buildings in this Third Generation PURE truck stop complex creates a striking contrast against the greenery, and the pale blue North Carolina sky. In the 1962 PURE Truck Stop Directory, the yet-to-become politically correct food services were listed as, "Restaurant (White & Colored)." Other services included, "mail pickup" and "ice service." The service garage at left must have been quite a challenge to work in during the winters.

Lannon's *Firebird* Truck Terminal

U.S. 17, FLA.-GA. LINE, RT. 1, YULEE, FLORIDA

P and N TRUCK STOP

1450 STATE ROAD #7, NORTH   •   WEST HOLLYWOOD, FLORIDA

Even as late as 1958, some PURE "Truck Stops" were nothing more than large-footprint gas stations. The Pem-7 Service Station was one. Although listed as a truck stop in the 1958 PURE TruckStation Directory, this station, located at the intersection of State Rd. 7 and Pembroke Rd. in West Hollywood, Florida, had listings that made it more of a gas station: Open 6:00am to 8:00pm; "Sleeping Facilities Near;" "Scales Near;" and "Restaurant Near." No mention of PURE's "Energee Diesel Fuel," only PURE-Pep and PURE Premium gasolines. By the time the 1960 PURE Truck Stop Directory had been printed, the Pem-7 was no longer listed. In 1962, the former Pem-7 re-emerges as the "P and N Truck Stop," sited in the exact same location. This shot displays the abstracted PURE cubical pylon and restaurant at center, flanked by a pair of circa-1960 Mack cabovers. Oddly, this truck stop was no longer listed in the 1965 PURE Truck Stop Directory.

H.R. and D. E. Whitehurst operated the Truckers Rest (PURE Truck Stop #219), located at 217 W. Ocean Drive on U.S. Highway 13 in Chesapeake, Virginia, from at least the early 1960s. A late 1940s GMC Cannonball cabover can be seen at left; a single truck service bay is at center just above the fuel attendant fueling the Studebaker; and the truckers' sleeping dorms are at right, on the second floor. Adequate signage advertises Steaks, Seafood, and Soda Fountain, amongst other amenities. As was often the case during this era, a clock is positioned prominently on the building's façade; orange neon "Truckers Rest" sits atop all.

Lannon's Firebird Truck Terminal (#651) was constructed in about 1963 on U.S. Highway 17, eight miles north of Yulee, Florida, at the Georgia/Florida state line, and was operated by Harry J. Lannon until about 1964 or '65 when Paul Sipe took over the reins. This shot highlights the sleeping facilities and abstracted PURE cubical form at center, and the restaurant at right. At left is a circa-late 1950s Mack B-61 conventional, and a circa-1960 Mack cabover.

The 29 Truck Stop is an excellent example of a truck stop built to resemble a First Generation roadside farmhouse. Sited on U.S. Highway 29 at Ruckersville, Virginia, this location began life as a TEXACO branded location and is seen elsewhere in this book as such. In this photo, we see it as it appeared about 1955. It was enlarged by 1957 and then replaced entirely about 1960 by a PURE Oil Co.-designed facility.

C. E. Welliver's Welliver Truck Stop (#643) dates from approximately 1960, and was located a mile east of Macon, Georgia, on U.S. Highways 129, 23, 80, and State Route 87. A circa-1956 Ford gas-powered tractor and trailer can be seen at left; the main building sports signage for "Restaurant," "Bar," "Pool Room," "Frozen Foods," "Gas," "Meats," "Feed," and a few other things. The 1961 and '62 PURE Truck Stop Directories note that there is restaurant seating for both "White and Colored." By 1962, this outlet was known as the "R & R Truck Stop;" by 1963, the R & R was being operated by J. W. Morris. J. H. Morris (J. W.'s son?) operated this truck stop from about 1965 until at least the early 1970s.

J. O. Weber's Pure Truck Stop (#716) was constructed in about 1960 at the intersection of U.S. Highways 82 and 49W, in Indianola, Mississippi. This aerial shot shows an expansive Chevrolet and Cadillac dealership at left (note the rooftop signage); ample paved parking and fuel islands; an abstracted PURE cubicle pylon at center; and restaurant at right. Dirt parking and service areas can be seen behind the main buildings. This location made the transition from Pure to Union in 1970 and was operating as late as 1972.

HICKS TRUCK STOP

U.S. 11 • WOODSTOCK, ALABAMA

Holland Truck Station

U.S. 50 AND 45   Flora, Illinois

Hick's PURE Truck Stop (#709), located on U.S. Highway 11 in Woodstock, Alabama, is a classic Second Generation truck stop: The site sports a large roadside frontage, with a relatively small overall footprint; sleeping facilities/showers at left ("Truckers Quarters"); restaurant at center; two-bay truck service building and fuel pumps further right—each service housed in its own separate building. By 1960, this outlet had become "Leuvada's," operated by Leuvada Daily; by 1962, Hick's was known as "Baggett's PURE Truck Stop" owned by J. B. Baggett and operated by George Mullens. This truck stop was no longer listed in the 1967 PURE Truck Stop Directory.

Bill Holland's "Holland Truck Station" (#316) dates from at least the late 1950s. Located at U.S. Highways 50 and 45 in Flora, Illinois, this shot shows the graveled approaches to the concrete fuel islands, but zero truck traffic; one might wonder if this could possibly be a pre-opening shot, as the restaurant windows at right seem to be covered inside by brown paper. This unit continued to operate as a PURE Truck Stop until at least the PURE conversion to Union 76 in the early 1970s.

GOWAN TRUCK CENTER

U.S. #82 . . . . Feeder Route U.S. #331-31-80-231

MONTGOMERY, ALABAMA

Dating from approximately 1960, the Gowan Truck Center (PURE Truck Stop #723) proudly shows off its meticulously graded gravel-dirt lot in this color photo. The lack of truck or auto traffic suggests that this might be a promotional shot, perhaps taken right before a Grand Opening. T. C. Gowan operated this attractive truck stop on U.S. Highway 82, near the intersection of Feeder Route U.S. 331, 31, 80, and 231, about one mile west of Montgomery, Alabama. By the early 1970s, PURE had renovated this site to a glass-encased abstraction of their Wildwood prototype, and was still owned by T. C. Gowan.

HATAM TRUCK STOP

780 S. CANAL ROAD — ROUTE 1 — DAYTONA BEACH, FLA.

Hatam's No. 1 Truck Terminal, (#614) located at 720 Canal Rd. on the U.S. Highway 1 Truck bypass in Daytona Beach, Florida, dates from at least the late 1950s, and was operated by Peter Hatam. The PURE central pylon has morphed into a specious slab, with prominent PURE signage visible at left, right, and over the fuel island office. Two open-air truck servicing bays can be seen at center; the restaurant is at right-center. Graveled approaches surround the concrete fuel islands. A 1948 Dodge can be seen fueling at center.

LEVEILLE'S BIG RIG TRUCKSTOP

15A BY-PASS • DE LAND, FLORIDA

2156

Dating from 1963, William D. Leveille's PURE Truck Stop #649, located at 15A bypass in De Land, Florida, offered the latest in the then-current truck stop technology. From left to right, an International conventional, a circa 1960 Mack cabover, a Diamond T conventional, and a B-61 Mack can be seen.

Bett's "Big T" truck stop was located on U.S. 19 at Chiefland, Florida, and in its early years sold GULF products and included a restaurant. After it became a PURE branded facility in the 1950s, it was enlarged and modernized.

Rebranded PURE before 1957, Betts' Big T Truck Stop (#632), located on U.S. Highway 19, two miles north of Chiefland, Florida, gets the message to its audience via an elaborate neon semi-truck sign at roadside: "On the Run it's Betts' Big T Service & Grill," the neon arrow points the way in. The expansive graveled-dirt lot features a brick-faced restaurant at left, a gas station and second-story dorm and showers facility to the right of it, and a service building to the right of the dorm. A circa-1950 GMC gas-powered tractor can be seen just to the left of the neon sign. This unit was operated by "Mrs. H. Betts" until about 1963, when Cecil R. Smith took over operations.

SUFFOLK TRUCK STOP, INC.

U.S. 13-460-58   Suffolk, Virginia

An apparent pre-Grand Opening photo taken in 1957 or slightly before. The concreted fuel islands and the pristine asphalt await their first customers at the Suffolk Truck Stop (#225), operated by Ralph Caldwell, located in Suffolk, Virginia. The lone circular PURE roadside sign, located near center, appears to be of incandescently-lighted porcelain-enamel variety. This truck stop was located at 624 E. Constance Rd., near the intersection of U.S. Highways 460, 58, and 13.

Bob's 82 Truck Stop (#724), owned by R. D. Scrivner, first shows up in the 1960 PURE Truck Stop Directory. This shot shows a meticulously-grade graveled-dirt lot, the pump islands, and a restaurant/showers/dormitory building. By the time the 1961 Directory was published, embellishments to the original structure had been added, including twin rooftop "PURE" neon signs (facing both up and down the highway); giant PURE lettering across the face of the second story wall facing the fuel islands; and a three-bay canopied service area behind the main building. At this point, Koss Courtney was the manager. This truck stop was located on the U.S. Highway 82 bypass, three miles west of Tuscaloosa, Alabama.

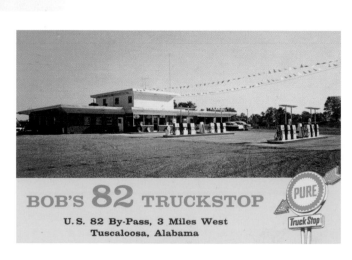

BOB'S 82 TRUCKSTOP

U.S. 82 By-Pass, 3 Miles West
Tuscaloosa, Alabama

JOHNSON'S ONE-STOP MOTOR SERVICE
U.S. #41-11-64 and Tenn. #58, Chattanooga, Tennessee

GATEWAY PURETRUCK STATION   West Memphis, Arkansas
Routes 61, 63, 64, 70 & 7

Johnson One Stop Motor Service (#722) was Douglas Johnson's 1960 entry into the truck stop business. Located in Chattanooga, Tennessee, at 1323 E. 23rd St. (U.S. Highways 41, 11, 64, and Tennessee bypass 58), this attractive outlet sat next to a freight terminal (right). Three of four diesel service bays can be seen at left; in approximately 1962, an expansion resulted in the construction of six additional bays. Restaurant and sleeping facilities can be seen to the right of the bays. Note the "Johnson's" proudly displayed in script on the abstracted PURE cube, and the Kendall Oil lollipop sign at roadside. This unit survived the Union 76 rebranding that occurred in the late 1960s-early '70s.

This attractive outlet was known as the Gateway PURE Truck Station, and was located at the junction of Highways 61, 63, 64, 70, and 79, in West Memphis, Arkansas. Three pump islands can be seen in this photo, each sporting three pumps. A graveled-dirt lot surrounds the main building, which sports a pseudo-pylon at left (with PURE spelled out in blue neon), beneath which a screen door is clearly visible. In front of the main building, a row of truck tires is book-ended by a soda ice chest at left, and a fuel pump on the right; a glass door flanks each, while further right is another screen door. The restaurant is to the left of (behind) the "pylon." The Chevy panel truck at left advertises the outlet on its rear door.

Mansfield Service Plaza (PURE Truck Stop #169) dates to approximately 1962, and was originally operated by Lyle W. Kohler. Located at the intersection of I-71 and Route 97 in Mansfield, Ohio, this unit originally sported the PURE signature blue neon over the sleeping facilities where the red neon-on-blue FOOD sign sits in this photo, and a PURE-OPEN sign beckoned truckers at roadside. That roadside signage was replaced in about 1963 with the signage shown in this photo. This photo also shows red neon-on-blue "Restaurant" arrow tacked on to second floor sleeping facilities, while a competing Howard Johnson's Restaurant and signage can be seen behind the twin service bays; A SUNOCO gas station is at far right. Late 1950s-early '60s White and International conventionals are at right.

Dale Gottbreht's PURE truck stop (#507) dates from at least 1957. Dale's was the most northerly (located 15 miles south of the Canadian border) and most westerly of the truck stops in PURE's truck stop chain, as well as PURE's only truck stop in North Dakota. By 1962, son George was operating the unit, which survived well into at least the early 1970s and eventually became a UNION 76 outlet. Note the snazzy Googie-style neon roadside signage at left. The PURE sign at center was changed from porcelain-enamel to plastic back-lit in about 1965.

Originally a PURE Cottage gas station, Craig & Nock's Restaurant at Diamond Springs in Norfolk, Virginia, had expanded to become this larger complex by the 1940s. By the late 1950s, it had become B and B Truck Center (#221), operated by C. B. "Bill" Bratten, and H. B. Bratten. By this time, Craig & Nock's Restaurant had morphed into a BBQ eatery. Located at U.S. Highways 13 and 13Y, 2 miles north of Norfolk, this truck stop was no longer featured in the 1966 PURE Truck Stop Directory, as a modern PURE service station was built at this location.

The Florida-Georgia Truck Terminal, located on U.S. Highway 1 at the Florida-Georgia state line dates to at least the late 1950s. PURE Truck Stop's outlet #622 was operated by Theodore Bussman during the mid 1960s, when this photo was taken. At left is a late 1950s Diamond T conventional. The PURE abstracted cube can be seen at center, with sleeping facilities to the left, and the restaurant to the right. There's icing facilities available in the distance between the two fuel islands.

MARKET TRUCK TERMINAL *U. S. Route #1 South of Ft. Pierce, Florida*

The Market Truck Terminal (#612) located on U.S. Highway 1, two miles south of Ft. Pierce, Florida, dates to at least 1957. Operated by Dave Cohan in the early 1960s, this shot displays the graveled approaches to the concrete fuel islands, with the fuel office and second floor sleeping facilities at center, and restaurant at right. Mr. Cohan (by now spelled, "Cohen" in the PURE Truck Stop Directories) was still operating the facility as of the early 1970s.

The Interstate Truck Terminal, Inc. (#635) dates to at least the 1957 PURE Truck Stop Directory. Operated by Doc Harper, this attractive truck stop shows off its restaurant at left, an abstracted PURE cube at center, and showers/dorm facilities just to the right of center. In this approximately 1958-dated photo, the approaches to the fuel islands are still in gravel. This outlet was located at U.S. Highways 301 and 321 North in Ulmers, South Carolina.

INTERSTATE TRUCK TERMINAL

U.S. 301 & 321   **ULMERS, SOUTH CAROLINA**

ALL STATE TRUCKSTOP
Interstate 75 and U.S. 41 • Unadilla, Georgia

Norwood Jackson opened the All State PURE Truck Stop (#661), located on I-75 at the U.S. Highway 41 interchange in about 1966. He was still operating it as a PURE/UNION 76 truck stop as of the early-to-mid 1970s.

TOMOKA RIVER TRUCK STOP

U.S. 1, 2 MILES NORTH - ORMOND BEACH, FLORIDA

The earliest appearance of the Tomoka River Truck Stop in Ormond Beach, Florida (#613), is in the 1957 PURE Truck Stop Directory. By 1963, the truck stop is missing from the Directory. In its final 1962 appearance, the truck stop was being operated by E. Carvill and R. Trombley. This shot shows the location sporting primarily late 1940s and early '50s autos. At left, in front of the service building (where one can purchase used tires for $2.00) sits what appears to be a 1948 Chevrolet pickup truck; at center is a blue and white 1956 Ford. The eatery is at far right. "General Repairing" is available 24 hours a day. Sealtest Ice Cream is offered at the restaurant. The approaches are graveled-dirt, but there is some asphalting visible at right.

Campbell's PURE Truck Center was located just north of the junctions of Interstate 81, and U.S. Highways 11 and 58 in Bristol, Virginia, and began life in about 1965 as PURE Truck Stop #740. Built in the typical cube design used for PURE truck stops in the early 1960s, the neon blue PURE signage once adorned the top of the sleeping facilities. In this photo, the oldest of this series of three, we see the site as it appeared shortly after it opened.

Campbell's Pure Truck Center

2701 Lee Highway – I-81 – U.S. 11 & 58
BRISTOL, VIRGINIA

Campbell's Union 76 Truck Center

2701 Lee Highway – I-81 – U.S. 11 & 58
BRISTOL, VIRGINIA

By the time this photo was taken about 1970, the PURE signage that originally was located on the cube had given way to the more carefree red "Campbell" signage as it appears in this photo. It appears that the facility had also been enlarged by the time this photo was taken. Ralph Hagy operated this outlet until the early 1970s, when operator Don Campbell took over.

Campbell's Truck Stop operated in the UNION 76 truck stop network until 1984. In this photo we see it in about 1980.

Everett G. Conrad's Better Truck Stop was a classy-looking little joint, all spiffy in its pure white and PURE blue tri-lined, neon-bedecked, finery. Located on Ohio Route 30 (The Lincoln Highway) at the intersection of Route 224, five miles west of Van Wert, Ohio, this was undoubtedly a heavily trafficked truck stop. While the approaches to the fuel island appear to be freshly asphalted, the Consolidated Freightways Freightliner sits in graveled-dirt, at left. This location offered a single diesel service bay, sleeping facilities, and showers; the sleeping facilities appear to be at left, behind the CF trailer. An International conventional tractor can be seen fueling at right, from one of the four late-1950s pumps on the twin fuel islands. A B-Model Mack at far right awaits its turn at the pumps.

YOUNG'S TRUCK SERVICE

U.S. 12 and 16
NORTH OF MAUSTON,
WISCONSIN

Bill Young operated his Young's Truck Service PURE Truck Stop (#519) from the late 1950s until about 1965, when it disappeared from the PURE Truck Stop directory. Located on Highways 12 and 16, three miles northwest of Mauston, Wisconsin, this shot highlights the carefully graded graveled lot, the sleeping facilities on the left, the restaurant on the right, and the fuel island office at center. Likely, this location continued as a truck stop after 1965, albeit rebranded to a competing brand.

Frank's Trucking Center occupied a prominent site at Bowers Hill, Virginia, for many years. Bowers Hill is a multiple highway junction (U.S. 13, U.S. 58, U.S. 460, at that time) where all of the roads leading west out of Norfolk-Portsmouth, Virginia, converge. Frank's was operating as early as 1957, and continues today as a Shell branded Convenience Store. In between, it was the most complete truck stop in eastern Virginia. Frank's operated a complete 24-hour truck service facility and had the first public scales in the area. It is seen here as it appeared in about 1967.

The Madison PURE Truck Stop (#307), operated by Ed Roets and Rex Grunewald, was a state-of-the-art Third Generation truck stop during the mid-1960s. Located at the intersection of I-90, I-94, and U.S. Highway 51 in Madison, Wisconsin, this truck stop epitomized the all-under-one-roof-type construction that defined the breed: fuel office at center; restaurant to the left; sleeping facilities above; two diesel service bays to the rear; four fuel pumps out front; expansive asphalted lot; plastic fluorescent roadside signage; and room to expand into the graveled truck parking area at the rear. Although a non-PURE corporate design, this truck stop had placed itself squarely into the Third Generation approximately four years prior to the opening of Wildwood.

This Carl A. Wright, Inc. PURE Truck Stop (#172) was located on Ohio State Route 29, one mile east of Celina, Ohio. Ray Grothouse operated this attractive facility from at least 1962. He was still operating it as of the early 1970s, at which time, sleeping facilities were being offered "nearby." The signage on this outlet is hard to miss; even the neon EAT sign at left, which appears to be facing away from the bulk of the traffic flow on Route 29.

Sometime around 1960 Al's Truck Stop joined the PURE truck stop network. It was located on U.S. 82 and U.S. 65 at Lake Village, Arkansas. Over the years, the facility expanded, and offered a complete motel, a restaurant, and garage facilities. This outlet made the transition to UNION 76 in 1970, and although downgraded to a "fuel stop" due to its non-Interstate location, continued to operate well into the 1980s. A Convenience Store occupies the site today.

KELLY'S PURE TRUCK PLAZA, MERIDIAN, MISSISSIPPI

Kelly's PURE Truck Plaza (#756), located at the junction of I-20 and I-59 in Meridian, Mississippi, was originally named "Meridian PURE Truck Stop" when it opened in about 1967. D. L. Kelly's operation advertised "Air Conditioned Sleeping Rooms With & Without Private Bath" as well as a "Large, Well-Stocked General Merchandise Store."

A more contemporary shot of the Holland Truck Station's roadside signage. Back in the days when the neon was blazing, it was surely a welcome call for tired truckers to pull off the two-lane for a bit of a respite.

A sorry state of decay for the Holland PURE Truck Station and its once-iconic roadside neon signage. This photo dates from the early 1990s.

This wide-angle shot of PURE's Wildwood, Florida (#656), truck stop displays all of the amenities that makes this a "Trucker's Paradise:" expansive asphalted parking and turn-arounds; multiple fuel lanes; Interstate Highway frontage; separation of auto and truck fueling facilities; and an overstated sleeping facilities/restaurant building at center. An early 1960s White "Japanese Freightliner" can be seen in this photo (left), as well as a Diamond T cabover (center), and a late '60s GMC DR-860 conventional (right).

JUPITER PURETRUCK STATION

U.S. 1 AND HOBE SOUND ROAD PURE JUPITER, FLORIDA

The Jupiter PureTruck Station (#808) dates from at least 1957. Located at the intersection of U.S. Highway 1 and Hobe Sound Rd., B. H. Gibson operated this truck stop until at least 1967, after which "Hugh" Gibson took over, followed by Grover Gibson by 1972. This outlet appears to have begun life as a gas station (center); a restaurant (at right) appears to have been added later. Finally, diesel pumps and a diesel service bay were added at a later date (at left).

In 1954 veteran truck stop operators Lee Speed and Bris Briscoe began construction of a new type of truck stop facility on U.S. 1 near Ashland, Virginia. Previously, they had operated service stations and truck stops in the Washington, D.C. area, and searched for a location where enough land was available for sufficient truck parking. In some other photos in this book, we see their U.S. 1 location under construction and in the early years of operation. After Interstate 95 bypassed the location in the 1960s, Speed and Briscoe built a new facility several miles from the original location but at an Interstate interchange. That facility made the transition to the UNION 76 brand, and is shown here as it appeared in the early 1970s. This unit continues to operate at this location today.

In 1966, the All State Truck Stop was opened in Unadilla, Georgia, by Norwood Jackson. Located along Interstate 75 at U.S. 41, this photo depicts the location as it appeared at about the time it opened. Construction was typical of the PURE designs of the 1960s for medium-sized locations.

Construction shot of Speed & Briscoe (PURE #210) in Ashland, Virginia. When it finally opened on December 30, 1954, this truck stop featured "Every Modern Convenience for the Trucker."

This stunning nighttime shot of Speed & Briscoe's shortly after opening shows the backlit PURE Oil Co. signature dark blue "Restaurant" and "Speed & Briscoe" signage displayed against the stark white of the concrete block building. Three uniformed pump jockeys await to service your vehicle while you dine in the casual confines of Nowland's Cafeteria. Three prominent signs remind auto drivers to "Park in the rear."

This rare interior shot of Nowland's Cafeteria, the restaurant facility located in the U.S. 1 Speed and Briscoe location, was used in PURE Oil Co. promotional material well into the 1960s.

This early shot of Speed & Briscoe's shows the location from across U.S. 1. The graded, graveled lot and the trucks date this shot to 1955 or so: At left sits a circa-1952 Mack H61T cabover; a late 1940s Mack conventional fuels at left-center; a circa-1953 Ford C-800 auto hauler can be seen at right. Workers have not yet completed installation of guardrail posts. Note the "air cooling" provided by the hinged open windows.

Nighttime shot of Speed & Briscoe, looking north, about 1955. Note the extensive use of area lighting all around the parking area.

A late 1940s Mack conventional fuels at Speed & Briscoe's gasoline pumps; diesel pumps were located out of the shot, left, closer to the highway.

This photo almost appears to be a Grand Opening shot. Suffolk, Virginia's Suffolk Truck Stop, Inc. (#225) dates from the late 1950s, and was located at 624 E. Constance Rd. at the intersection of Highways 13, 460, and 58. Ralph Caldwell's 1965 PURE Truck Stop Directory listing shows sleeping facilities as part of this operation, but it is hard to determine from this photo where they might be located. Apparently, this location survived the late 1960s conversion from PURE to UNION 76, still operated by Mr. Caldwell. Note the absence of any type of PURE abstracted cube on the building.

In the fall of 1967 a new PURE truck stop opened at Interstate 94 and Ruan Rd. in Milwaukee, Wisconsin. This aerial photo shows the scale and scope of truck stop design as it reached its peak in the 1960s. Note the massive paved parking lot, and the inclusion of all facilities under one roof, seen here at the time of the grand opening in late 1967.

In 1965, Romer ("Bill"), Richard ("Dick"), and Robert ("Bob") Burns opened their PURE Cincinnati South Truck Plaza (#193) at I-75 and State Route 18, on the Burlington Pike, in Florence, Kentucky. As was typical of Third Generation Truck Stops, separation of truck and auto traffic is evidenced by twin signage delineating a "Truck Entrance" and a "Car Entrance." At left can be seen an early 1960s GMC Crackerbox cabover, and an International Emeryville cabover.

Frazeyburg, Ohio's Route 16 Truck Stop (#117) was located on Route 16 and Carlisle Rd. West, and was PURE branded from at least 1957, although this photo appears to be of a slightly later vintage. Possibly a First Generation Truck Stop that survived into the Third Generation era, a photo in a 1958 PURE Truck Stop Directory shows a neon clock located at the roofline of this likely roadside farmhouse where the neon EAT sign is approximately located in this shot. This location was open "24 hours" (except for being closed from 2:00pm Saturday to 2:00pm Sunday), and was operated by Bob Patton in 1960. There is no mention of sleeping facilities being available. This unit apparently survived in the PURE chain (albeit sans photos in their Truck Stop Directories) until the mid-1970s, still operated by Bob Patton. And even then, the hours were still the same.

An opposite-angle shot of Frazeyburg, Ohio's Route 16 Truck Stop. That's a mid-1950s GMC conventional fueling. Note the graveled lot, and the signage advertising "Powell's Barber Shop," at right.

The Dixie Way truck stop is an example of a roadside service station promoting itself as a truck stop. Located on U.S. 25, the Dixie Highway, in Rudolph, Ohio, these two classic scenes show the location at it appeared about 1956.

This fueling emporium at the intersection of Ohio State Routes 15 and 20A typify the 1950s and '60s rural truck stop. Located three miles east of Montpelier, Ohio, Simon Siler, Jr.'s Ace Truck Stop (#158) could easily have begun its life as a gas station, with pumps on the front side of the building, then expanded by adding diesel pumps at left, a restaurant (beneath cute little candy-striped awnings), and a pair of diesel pumps (at right—not visible in this photo). A Fritos truck fuels at right; further right is a late 1940s GMC Norwalk van. The only paving for this entire Second Generation truck stop is the concrete surrounding the fuel islands. The 1961 PURE Truck Stop Directory lists sleeping facilities as being "near;" no mention is made of shower facilities. The second shot appears to have been taken from the backside of the facility, as all PURE blue neon-letter signage faces away from the photographer. The "Grill Meats" delivery truck is the latest vehicle in this photo and dates from at least 1959. The two photos show the relatively diminutive size of this outlet.

The Cabin Creek Truck Stop was located at the fork of a critical highway junction, at U.S. 1 and U.S. 52 outside Cheraw, South Carolina. Although directory listings indicate that this facility offered a restaurant and sleeping facilities, no such facilities are evident in this photo. After dropping out of the truck stop program around 1960, a PURE service station operated here for many years. This shot is from about 1956.

The Hi-Way Truck Stop was located along U.S. 460 east of Princeton, West Virginia, and was an early addition to the PURE truck stop network. By all appearances, this truck stop came to life when a relatively modern restaurant was grafted on to an existing country store. This photo shows the location in about 1962.

Located along Interstate 94 at Sawyer, Michigan, the Sawyer Truck Plaza (PURE Truck Stop #384) was operated by Dick Richardson. Built to the latest standards of the day, this Third Generation truck stop included individual sleeping rooms with individual bathrooms, scales, a large truckers' store, and an on-site barber shop, all amenities that truckers were seeking in new stops of the 1960s. It is shown here in about 1967.

The J & J Truck Stop (#132) dates as PURE branded facility from at least 1957. This truck stop was located on U.S. Highway 21, midway between Charleston and Parkersburg, West Virginia. The porcelain-enamel PURE signage at the pumps is augmented by a plastic back-lit PURE sign at right, with signage below that offers a "Discount for Trucks." John R. Simmons operated this facility at the time this photo was taken in the late 1950s, and was still listed as the operator by the time the PURE rebranding to UNION 76 was completed in the early 1970s.

Wayne F. Gibson's Capital City Truck Stop (PURE Truck Stop #238), 10 miles north of Raleigh, North Carolina, on U.S. Highway 1. It is shown here in a grand opening photo from 1961. In the 1962 PURE Truck Stop Directory, the yet-to-become politically correct food services were listed as, "Restaurant (White & Colored)." Other services included, "mail pickup" and "ice service." The service garage at left must have been quite a challenge to work in during the winters. A restaurant operated here until relatively recent times.

At the time these photos were taken, about 1960, the 117 PURE Truck Stop had just been rebuilt into the modern facility shown here. A PURE branded truck stop had operated here for several years, and after it was taken over by Osborne Parks, the facility went through a modernization. In the late 1960s, it was modified further, by adding sleeping facilities enlarging the repair garage. It was located on U.S. 117 at the southern entrance to Goldsboro, North Carolina, and operated throughout the UNION 76 era, becoming a Shell branded facility in the 1990s, before closing in about 2005.

The Road King truck stop opened in 1961 on U.S. 15-401 outside Laurinburg, North Carolina. In this instance the facility was constructed from a basic prefabricated steel structure of the style typical for industrial facilities of that era. Included in the main facility was a coin-operated laundry along with sleeping facilities and showers, as well as the usual eatery. It is shown here at about the time that it opened.

An overhead shot of Leveille's Big Rig Truck Stop (#649) in De Land, Florida. A Late 1950s GMC DR-Series tractor-trailer can be seen exiting the lot at left; a late 1950s Mack cabover fuels at right. An open-air service "garage" sits behind the main building, with graveled parking available behind it. The abstracted PURE cube form at center serves only as a signboard for the neon blue PURE signage.

In the early 1990s, UNION 76 announced that it would discontinue marketing in the southeastern U.S. Former UNION jobbers banded together and licensed the PURE brand from UNION, and overnight PURE signage went up in 10 southeastern states. A restriction in the arrangement prevented the PURE brand from appearing on truck stops operated by the group. Horn's Travel Plaza had opened in the early 1970s on Interstate 40 at U.S. 601 in Mocksville, North Carolina, and had operated as a UNION 76 truck stop from the time it opened until the program was discontinued. Horn's then joined the Ambest network, and while the PURE restriction existed, branded the operation as Shell. After the restriction was lifted in the mid 2000s, the owner, local PURE jobber Horn Oil Company, branded the facility to PURE, as it exists today. Here it is in the summer of 2010.

After the success of the first-ever, designed-from-the-ground-up truck stop at Imlay City, Michigan, Hickok Oil Co. began looking for other opportunities to expand their food and fuel concept. In 1939, in Jackson, Michigan, the company built the first station of the design shown here. In addition to Hi-Speed gasoline and oils, this station featured a two-bay service area and a full restaurant. In a separate group of buildings, a 12-room motel was available to both tourists and truckers. This design was so successful that seven of these stations were built in Michigan and Ohio before WWII interrupted. It is seen here at the time it opened in late 1939.

PURE Oil Co. Subsidiaries

Hickok Oil Co.

• Founded in Toledo, Ohio, in 1917; originators and operators of the Hi-Speed brand.

• Hickok's first branded gas station was opened at the corner of Detroit and Glenwood Streets in Toledo. Additional gas stations were opened in other Ohio cities, and also in Michigan.

• The PURE Oil Co. purchased initial interests in Hickok in 1928. At the time, Hickok had grown to nearly 280 gas stations. The purchase was competed by PURE in 1951.

• Hickok designed and operated several gas stations that featured a centralized tower as a defining architectural feature. This tower was implemented as a prominent attribute in Hickok's, and indeed the world's, first "gas station for trucks." Hickok's premier "truck stop" debuted in 1935 in Imlay City, Michigan, at the intersection of Michigan Highways 21 and 53.

• *Number of confirmed Hickok branded truck stops operating in the U.S.:* Further truck stop development continued during the 1940s, and Hi-Speed was in the process of branding 28 truck stops, when, in 1952, the brand was replaced by PURE. Afterward, PURE successfully marketed Hickok's truck stop concept on a scale that resulted in a chain of nearly 350 PURE branded truck stops during a period between the late 1950s and the late 1960s, after having fully acquired Hickok in the early 1950s.

Shell Oil Co.

• Began retail marketing of gasoline in the U.S. in 1912 as the American Gasoline Co. with the purchase of a terminal in Washington state.

• Through acquisitions, Shell was marketing fuels at the retail level in all states by 1929.

• After having been in and out of certain marketing areas over the past 80 years, Shell has remained a consistent marketer, and for many years was the retail sales leader of gasoline in the U.S., although never a leader in the number of outlets.

Truck Stop Operations

Number of confirmed Shell branded truck stops operating in the U.S. by year:

1968: 187

Due to market conditions, Shell's retail marketing areas expanded and contracted dramatically several times between the mid-1930s and mid-1990s. Total Shell branded operating truck stops ranged from the upper 40s in the early '70s to the lower 40s by 1984.

1995: 13

Smith's Truck Stop is an example of where a country store operator was situated along a strategic highway, and after adding fuel to their product mix, promoted themselves as a truck stop. Despite its small size, Smith's advertised home cooked meals and bunks for truckers. Shell products were sold at this location, along U.S. 21 north of Columbia, South Carolina. It was photographed here in about 1960.

U.S. 301 is a major north-south highway, and truck stops can be found throughout its length. One such location was the 301 Truck Stop, a facility in Fayetteville, North Carolina, developed by the local Shell jobber. Restaurant and garage facilities were available, and although not advertised, it appears that a dormitory was located upstairs; an ice dock sits out beyond the main building. The older photo dates from about 1956, when the facility was relatively new; the later photo below shows the same location in about 1965.

U.S. Highway 58 across southern Virginia tied the population centers of Norfolk and vicinity to the major north-south routes, as well as to U.S. 1 and U.S. 301 that ran inland from the coastal cities. The road saw heavy truck traffic during the buildup of Tidewater's military facilities before WWII, and continues as a major trucking route today. Bryant's One Stop Inn was located on U.S. 58 just west of Suffolk, Virginia. Operated by Collis and Mabel Bryant, the design is typical of First Generation truck stops. Because supplying the military bases was a one-way ride for truckers, the Bryants were some of the first truck stop operators to focus on seeking return loads for their customers. Shell products were sold here when photographed in 1959.

Shack's "19 Truck Stop" was located on U.S. 19 at Fanning Springs, Florida, and was a companion facility to Shack's "301-1 Truck Stop" on the 301 Highway in northern Florida. The two constructions were nearly identical, but Shell products were sold at Fanning Springs, while Cities Service products were sold at the northern location. They advertised free air-conditioned sleeping rooms for truckers, presumably with a minimum fuel purchase. This location is seen as it appeared in about 1955.

The Shell Dieselene pump was located conveniently at the Cross Roads Truck Stop, at the intersection of U.S. 31W and State Route 65 in Park City, Kentucky. It appears that this location began life as a regular service station, but with the addition of a restaurant on one end of the station, and a motel elsewhere on the lot, they began promoting themselves as a truck stop. It is shown here as it appeared in about 1960.

Another truck stop along U.S. 301 was Honeycutt's, a Shell branded facility at Lucama, North Carolina. It appears that an existing service station was expanded by adding a restaurant to the original structure. At the time of this 1965 photo, the Interstate 95 section that would eventually bypass this location had not yet been built, and truck stops could be found all along the highway. After I-95 was built, numerous truck stops were built at Kenly, North Carolina, just south of this location, and the old highway locations were phased out.

The Dells Oasis Truck-O-Tel was a jobber-developed truck and travel stop at the Lake Delton, Wisconsin, exit off Interstate 90-94. In this 1965 photo we see a then-modern construction featuring a large restaurant and up-to-date fueling facility. This location served as a Greyhound stop for many years, as well.

Bruno's Oil Co., Shell distributor in the Swan River, Minnesota, area, operated this truck stop at the junction of U.S. 2 and U.S. 65 east of Grand Rapids, Minnesota. As always, a café was one of the fixtures, and propane was available for refrigeration units. It is seen here as it appeared in about 1964.

Noble's Truck Stop began life as a diner along U.S. 17 south of Chocowinity, North Carolina, but with the addition of a Shell gas station with oversized service bays and an ice dock, they began promoting themselves as a truck stop. The lot included an incredible amount of parking, which no doubt contributed to the truck stop's success. It is seen here in about 1966.

Heath's Cafe and Truck Stop
U. S. 17
10 Miles North of New Bern, N. C.

Another, much older Shell branded truck stop on U.S. 17 between New Bern and Chocowinity, North Carolina, was Heath's. Heath's had its origins as a restaurant and motor court in the 1930s, and with the addition of truck service following WWII they began promoting the location as a truck stop. It is seen here as it appeared in the late 1940s. This writer has traveled that road regularly for years, and no remnants of this facility are evident today.

Cabover Macks are parked to allow their drivers a rest stop at this Shell branded facility. Sadly, the location has been lost to history.

The Red Hot Truck Stop was located along U.S. 11, 45 and 80 on the bypass around Meridian, Mississippi. Typical of roadside businesses of the era, the Red Hot was advertised with elaborate oversized signage. Sinclair products were being sold here when photographed about 1957. Note the extensive graveled lot.

Sinclair Oil Co. and Affiliates

Sinclair Oil & Refining Corp.
• Founded in 1916 in New York City, New York.
• A series of acquisitions during the 1920s and 1930s gave Sinclair coast-to-coast marketing in the U.S.
• Purchased Covey's Little America Refining Co. (LARCO) in 1955. At the time, Little America was the world's largest gas station and truck stop, with 55 pumps.
• Merged with ARCO in 1969.
• Sinclair was sold to independent marketer Earl Holding in 1976, son-in-law of S. M. Covey, originator of the LARCO and Mobile brands, and current owner of the Little America Resorts chain.

Truck Stop Operations
• *Number of confirmed Sinclair branded truck stops operating in the U.S. by year:*
1960: 126 (Including the Richfield Oil Co. of New York branded truck stops)
1964: 142 (An additional approximately 660 locations are identified as gas stations that also sell diesel fuels).
1970: 187
From the early 1970s until 1998, confirmed Sinclair branded truck stops increased and decreased dramatically from as few as approximately 20 to as many as 45.

Peterson's Super Service was located on U.S. 30 in Fremont, Nebraska, and had expanded from a simple roadside service station with the addition of a restaurant and diesel fuel islands. This photo dates from about 1960.

Bill's is an example of the new generation of truck stops that were being built in the early 1960s. Located on the frontage road along Interstate 85 just south of Lexington, North Carolina, Bill's was a prefabricated structure that encompassed all services in one building. Sinclair products were being sold here when photographed in about 1964, and various other brands have been sold there since that time. It remains in operation today, and still appears much as seen here.

Hine's is a classic truck stop of the 1950s. Bunks in a second floor bunkhouse are available, along with restaurant and fueling facilities. Hine's was located along U.S. 40 and 127 at Eaton, Ohio, and was photographed here in about 1955.

Produce Truck Stop advertised "Everything for Truckers," and among their many amenities, one could find air-conditioned bunk space, showers, scales, LPG, and complete mechanical services. It was located on the U.S. 17 truck route in Jacksonville, Florida, and was photographed here in about 1955.

Complete restaurant and service station accommodations of the highest type, designed especially for motorists. Service and facilities unexcelled in metropolitan areas.

The Pennant Taverns were early roadside tourist stops developed by Pierce Oil Co. in the late 1920s. The sites included rooms, a restaurant and store, and gas stations. When Pierce Oil was purchased by Sinclair in the early 1930s, Sinclair continued to operate the facilities. The example shown in these photos was built in 1928 and was located on U.S. 63 and 66 in Rolla, Missouri. It was photographed here in about 1933. Other Pennant Taverns could be found in Columbia and Springfield, Missouri, as well as in Tulsa, and Miami, Oklahoma.

Richfield Oil Co. of New York

- Founded in 1929 when Richfield Oil Co. of California purchased Walburn Petroleum Co. and Acewood Petroleum Co., both of New York City.
- In 1935, bankruptcy forced the sale of Richfield of New York; Sinclair purchased the operations from Richfield of California, and continued to operate the company as a secondary brand until 1964, when Richfield of New York was dissolved, and all retail outlets were rebranded to Sinclair.
- From 1937 until the late 1950s, Richfield operated 100% through jobbers. It is likely that some of these jobbers operated locations that they considered to be truck stops, but no real effort was made to organize them with any truck stop program.
- As of 1960, truck stops that were considered part of the Sinclair Truck Stop network were operating in Ernul, North Carolina; Duncansville, Pennsylvania; and throughout Massachusetts and were all branded Richfield of New York. These would be rebranded to Sinclair in 1964.

Little America Refining Co.(LARCO)

- Founded in 1933 in the Salt Lake City area as the Covey Gas and Oil Co. by S. M. Covey, his wife Grace Christy Papworth (Covey), and several family members who were blood relatives to the Call family, originators of the Flying J chain of gas stations and truck stops.
- Covey Gas and Oil marketed "Mobile" brand fuels, utilizing a 1920s-style (and later '40s) racing car as a logo.
- The company's flagship location was "Little America Wyoming," built in the early-1930s. It was located near Granger, Wyoming, on the north side of the Lincoln Highway near its junction with Highway 30N (locally known as "Granger Junction"). It sported twin gas pumps, 12 cabins, and a 23-seat café and ice cream parlor.
- Within a decade, Little America Wyoming had expanded, straddling The Lincoln Highway, to include perhaps as many as eight fuel pumps; a dance floor/cocktail lounge ("The Palm Room"), a restaurant, and additional rooms in a hotel, all located in a two-story building sited on the south side of the Highway.
- The original location was destroyed by fire in 1949, and a new Little America was built a short distance from the original location, featuring a restaurant, a

In one early incarnation, the amenities that Covey's Little America offered on the north side of its straddle of the Lincoln Highway featured a total of six gas pumps, including two 1920s-era visible-register models, and four clock-faced computing types. Five of those pumps were situated under a couple of pseudo-canopies that offered minimal protection from the elements. The larger of the two canopies was topped by a huge horizontally-oriented neon sign featuring a speeding 1930s race car touting Covey Gas & Oil Co. products; the smaller island was bedecked with a vertically-oriented neon sign featuring a plethora of penguins, and a trio of spot lights, topped by a flagpole. Behind the larger of the two pump islands was the Soda Fountain, to the right of which was perhaps a total of five tourist court-type rooms (the "Lodge"). Note the extensive use of the Streamline Moderne architectural style on the main building with the rounded corners on the windows, the porthole on the restroom door, and the "speed lines" encircling the crown of the Soda Fountain building and the pump canopies. A couple of 1920s-era flivvers can be seen at extreme left, and just to the right of the main pump island.

A late-1940s shot of Covey's Little America, looking west: Main roadside signage at left, motel facilities to the right of the sign, with the main restaurant/gift shop building at left center. Covey's Mobile branded gas station is at center (with "Covey's Mobile Gasoline, Beautiful Rest Rooms" neon signage atop), sporting 10 pumps with station-lighters and a single auto service bay. More lodging can be seen behind the gas station building. A driver tends to his Diamond T tractor, at right.

In 1949, Little America suffered a catastrophic fire. Owner S. M. Covey rebuilt at a slightly more southerly location, as the Lincoln Highway, on which his operation had been sited, had by then been realigned. This aerial shot from the 1950s shows the motel buildings at left; the main building at left-center (which housed the coffee shop, the dining room, the gift shops, the cocktail lounge, the bus stop, the soda fountain, and the restrooms); the fueling facilities at right-center (which at this point did not feature all of the 55 pumps for which the truck stop would later be known); and what appears to be a flat-roofed, two-bay truck servicing building at right. To the further right sits four diesel pumps and a five-tank bulk fuel storage facility. Additional motel rooms (for a total of 115 at this point) can be seen behind the gas station building. Because of the severe Wyoming winters, a large percentage of Little America's employees lived on-site, presumably in the other extraneous buildings located towards the back of the property. In the 1960s, I-80 would run a bit further south, towards the bottom of the photograph, and would provide ample off-ramps for travelers wishing to visit "The World's Largest Gas Station" and truck stop.

Looking east in this circa late-1940s photo, we can see the main restaurant/gift shop building at Covey's Little America. Neon building signage advertises, "Beautiful Rest Rooms," "Motor Lodges," "Cocktail Lounge," and "Coffee Shop." Day rooms are available from 8:30am to 4:30pm for travelers needing a quick nap and a shower before returning to the two-lane.

coffee shop, a cocktail lounge and bar, motel rooms, and a service station, selling diesel fuel also. This location became a favorite stopover for truckers, due to it being the only road-related service stop along a lengthy, isolated stretch of highway.

• The corporate name was changed from Covey Gas and Oil to LARCO (Little America Refining Co.) in the early 1950s.

• In 1952, S. M. Covey turned over operation of Little America to son-in-law Earl Holding and his wife Carol.

• The Sinclair Oil & Refining Co. purchased Covey's LARCO operations in 1955. At the time, Little America Wyoming was the world's largest gas station

The flat-roofed, two-bay truck service building depicted in the 1950s aerial shot has been either remodeled or replaced with a gabled-roofed, three-bay building by the time this photo of Little America was taken in the early 1960s. There are 25 truckers' gas and diesel pumps displayed here, although probably at least five more are hidden by the orange Allied Van Lines truck. A Global Van Lines Dodge conventional can be seen to the left of the Allied trailer, and a Mayflower Van Lines GMC can be seen at far left. As was the practice at the time, this self-proclaimed "Queen of The Highways" travel center offered no intentional separation of truckers and motorists within the restaurant/gift shop buildings, or the motel.

This early-1960s photo of Little America reveals that the outlet now advertises as being owned by neither the Covey's nor the Holding's. Note that additional lodging has been added at far left.

In the 1940s, Little America sported eight gasoline pumps. This photo shows an expansion to 12 (center); by the late 1960s, that number had been increased to 15. However, there are at least 22 diesel and gasoline pumps (at right) exclusively for truckers, offered in this shot. An early-1950s Pacific Intermountain Express Peterbilt appears to be headed for the truck parking at the rear of the lot. Note that the rooftop race car sign now advertises, "Sinclair Gasoline" and that the main Little America signage near center displays neither the Covey nor the Holding name.

The Holding family, daughter and son-in-law of Little America originator S. M. Covey, now operate Little America in this mid-1960s photo. No longer are the "Beautiful Restrooms," "Motor Lodges," "Cocktail Lounge," and "Coffee Shop" advertised in neon on the side and front of the main building, as was done 20 years earlier. The sign beneath the main signage that, in the 1940s, advertised the availability of Day Rooms, now advertises that 310 miles to the east, in Cheyenne, a second Holding's Little America facility beckons. Reservations can be made for free!

and truck stop, operating 55 fuel pumps. The station was rebranded from Mobile to Sinclair.

• S.M. Covey died in 1959.

• In 1967, Earl Holding purchased a mothballed Mobil Oil Co. refinery in Casper, Wyoming, to supply the original Little America, Wyoming travelers' stop, as well as newly-opened resorts located in Cheyenne, and Salt Lake City. The Cheyenne location operated 50 fueling pumps, but billed itself more as a resort than a truck stop even though adequate truck parking was provided. The Salt Lake City operation was simply a motel and gas station, which was later replaced by a multi-story resort hotel.

• In 1976, Holding's Little America chain purchased the Sinclair Oil Co., expanding the enterprise from a small chain of regional truck stops and resorts into a large oil distribution company with a marketing area covering most of the western U.S. Additional Little America branded resorts have been built in Flagstaff, Arizona, and Sun Valley, Idaho, as well as San Diego, California.

• Little America, Wyoming, remains as the chain's only dedicated truck stop, although some consider the Cheyenne location to be a second truck stop, and the Sinclair website currently lists the Flagstaff resort as a "truck stop." The chain is still operated by the Holding Family.

In Cheyenne, Wyoming, 310 miles east of the original Little America, the Holding's opened a second "Travel Center" (as it was billed). Although more of a resort, it was neither intended nor designed to be specifically a truck stop. Swimming pools, meeting rooms, a golf course, and banquet and convention facilities were all part of the picture now, foreshadowing the direction the Holding's would take as they were striving to become more of a hotelier/resort complex operator. In this obviously retouched photo, the roadside signage should read, "Holding's," not "Holding." Additionally, the top panel is actually red, not black, the bottom panel is blue, and the lettering is white, not red. The Sinclair station is state-of-the-art late 1960s.

Looking eastward in this late-1960s photo, Holding's Little America now advertises that they are the "World's Largest Service Station—55 Pumps," and touts their Sinclair gasoline branding. A rare Dodge CN-900 tractor-trailer rig can be seen in the parking lot, at right.

This north-facing aerial shot shows a mid-1980s-era Little America. At upper left are the housing facilities for the employees who live on-site. Paved parking has been expanded, and additional motel rooms have been constructed, reaching westward. Running out of the picture at right center is the original two-lane that once fronted Little America; at the bottom of the photo is the current I-80 and concomitant underpasses needed to reach the facility now.

HOTEL: In one early incarnation, the amenities that Covey's Little America offered on the south side of its straddle of the Lincoln Highway featured a hotel (on the second floor), about a half-dozen cabins in a "Lodge," a couple of early 1930s clock-faced gas pumps, a coffee shop, a cocktail lounge, a bar, and a dance floor ("The Palm Room"). Again, the Streamline Moderne architectural styling is apparent with the inclusion of porthole windows, round-top windows in the doors, the speed lines encircling the crest of the upper floor and the pump island canopy, and even in the porthole on the leading edge of the huge neon signage over the fuel pumps. One wonders about the viability of live palm trees growing so vibrantly in the harsh Wyoming winter weather, especially so many, so uniformly, so close to a building that shields the southerly sun… STRADDLING THE LINCOLN HIGHWAY: Before the disastrous fire which precipitated a rebuilding of Little America along the 1940s alignment of the Lincoln Highway, Little America looked like this. Straddling the 1913 alignment of The Lincoln, a cocktail lounge/dance floor ("The Palm Room"), coffee shop, bar, second story hotel rooms, and a pair of gas pumps occupied the north-facing facility (left). The south-facing facility (right) featured four additional fuel pumps, restrooms, ice cream/soda fountain, and a "lodge" featuring a half-dozen or so motel-type rooms. Note the speeding race car rooftop signage touting Covey Gas & Oil Co's. "Quality Products." A "Chicken in the Rough" dinner (five pieces of chicken, shoestring potatoes, biscuits, and honey, intended to be eaten by hand, without utensils) was 55 cents, and lunch ranged from 40 to 60 cents, according to the sign, just left of center. LODGE: Before the 1949 fire which ultimately resulted in Covey's Little America being moved to a location further south, the lodging facilities consisted of a half-dozen or so rooms located in this "Lodge" situated on the north side of the Lincoln Highway. Note the penguin motif atop the entrance.

Skelly Oil Co.

• Founded in Tulsa, Oklahoma, 1919 by William Grove Skelly.

• The Skelly Oil Co. was controlled by the Standard Oil Co. of New Jersey during The Depression, after Skelly defaulted on some of Standard's loans.

• Skelly was later controlled by The Mission Corp., which was created by Standard specifically for operating its Skelly and Tidewater operations.

• The Mission Corp. was purchased by J. Paul Getty in 1937.

• Getty retained majority interest in Skelly until its inevitable merger with the Getty Oil Co. in 1977.

• In 1983 the Getty name began replacing the Skelly name at Skelly stations throughout the Midwest. However, before the conversion was complete, Getty Oil was purchased by TEXACO. TEXACO converted select Skelly locations to the TEXACO brand, including much of their truck stop network. Other locations were caught in the middle of the rebranding, which was never completed. Independently-owned stations would continue to display abandoned Skelly and Getty signage for many years.

Truck Stop Operations

• The Skelly Truck Stop Program was begun in 1960. Locations for "Approved Skelly Truck Stops" were chosen as far west as the Rocky Mountains, as far north as the Canadian Border, and as far south as the Mexican Border and the Gulf Coast.

• Skelly continued to operate independently until about 1983, when Skelly outlets began being rebranded to Getty.

• Before the Skelly-to Getty rebranding was completed, Getty sold the Skelly operation to TEXACO in 1984. At that time, all Skelly operations were rebranded to TEXACO, and The Skelly Oil Co. ceased to exist.

• *Number of confirmed Skelly branded truck stops operating in the U.S. by year:*

1958: 40
1960: 60
1961: 48
1962: 48
1963: 116
1966: 166
1967: 165
1968: 175
1969: 200
1972: 207
1975: 217
1977: 193
1979: 196
1981: 190

The windswept plains of eastern Wyoming were the home of E. W. Goodrich's Skelly Big Wheel Truck Stop (T-204), located at the junction of I-25 and U.S. Highway 20, 1.5 miles east of Douglas. Most striking about this otherwise ordinary Third Generation truck stop are the triple spikes thrusting from atop the restaurant; Skelly Big Wheel Truck Stop/Restaurant neon signage is mounted on these spikes, and is unique to this truck stop in the Skelly Truck Stop chain. This location was constructed sometime prior to 1966, when such neon extravaganzas were still relatively the norm. An early-1960s Kenworth cabover fuels near center.

Rapid City, South Dakota's Skarty Oil Co. and Sioux Oil Co. teamed up to open Rapid I-90 Truck Stop (T-245), located at the intersection of I-90 and State Highway 79, in January of 1968. On Saturday and Sunday, May 3rd and 4th, 1968, Managers Roy and Arlean Crow held a Grand Opening that included free coffee, soft drinks, donuts, and ice cream cones for all. Radios, BBQs, tires, gasoline, and steak dinners were given away in drawings. In keeping with the Third Generation truck stop "separation of traffic" trend, separate drawings were held for motorists and truckers, with "truckers only" being allowed for a special drawing of a Sony TV. This shot shows a cabover Kenworth flatbed fueling at the fuel islands during the Grand Opening days.

ANDERSON TRUCK STOP

H. ELLS OIL CO. AND CAFE
24 HOUR TRUCK STOP
HEBRON, NEBRASKA, ON HIGHWAY 81

As you entered Bowman, North Dakota, on U.S. Highway 12 in the late 1950s, you would be greeted by this American Indian bow man sign. This postcard for Anderson's Town & Country Truck Stop (T-142), operated by Robert L. Anderson, inadvertently also advertises a competing Mobil outlet, just to the right of the sign. The brick-façade building offers the Town & Country Café at left, auto service bays at center, with fuel islands at right, and truck service bay behind. Fuel island and parking in front of the café are paved in concrete, while the approaches are graveled. The café features stylish late-1950s linoleum flooring, tubular-framed chairs, and an inviting counter with stools. Sleeping facilities come in the form of the 4U Motel, located across the highway.

H. Ells Oil Co. operated this Skelly Truck Stop (T-188) in Hebron, Nebraska, located at the intersection of U.S. Highways 81 and 136, as early as 1963. The expansive brick service building sporting café, fuel office, and two service bays all under one roof identify this as an early Third Generation truck stop. The three fuel pumps nearest the building are late 1950s-era globe-topped units; those closest to roadside are early '60s-era, sans globes. The predominant ice cream signage, the planter boxes in front of the café and the blinds within, further assert the return to "domesticity," another characteristic in the design of the Third Generation truck stop. The back of the postcard from which this image was taken advertises an additional H. Ells location: "Ells Skelly Truck Stop – York, Nebr." That location does not show up in the Skelly Truck Stop Directories until 1968, and even then, it is known as, "Crossroads Skelly" (F-083), a Fuel Stop operated by Lawerence Baldwin. By 1978, H. Ells' T-188 truck stop ceased to be a Skelly branded outlet.

BELLE TRUCK STOP
JCT. HIGHWAYS U. S. 85 & 34 — 1 MILE SOUTH
BELLE FOURCHE, SOUTH DAKOTA

Arlis "Buck" Binney managed the Bell Truck Stop (T-181) from the early 1960s until at least 1977. Located 3/4 of a mile south of Belle Fourche, South Dakota, at the intersection of U.S. Highway 85 and State Route 34, this shot displays the Belle's single service bay at left, and the fuel islands and false-front office at center. Restaurant and sleeping facilities are out of the photo, at right. A mid-1950s Diamond T cattle truck fuels at right. The entire lot is gravel, save for the concrete fuel islands. By 1978, this outlet was no longer listed in the Skelly Truck Stop Directories.

Even before there was a Skelly Truck Stop network, there were truck stops that sold Skelly products. Ernie's Truck Stop was one such establishment, and was located on U.S. 12 at Mauston, Wisconsin. Features included a restaurant and dormitory, along with load-locator services. There is no Skelly signage visible, but there is a neat "Gas for Less" neon arrow at roadside, complemented by "Ernie's" and "EAT" neon atop the buildings. One can only guess at what the "Motor Cargo" and "KAT" signage on the light standard at right refers to. This photo dates from about 1955. It had either closed or rebranded before Skelly developed their truck stop program, as it does not appear in any directories.

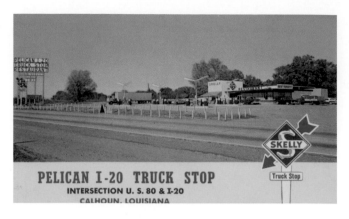

PELICAN I-20 TRUCK STOP
INTERSECTION U. S. 80 & I-20
CALHOUN, LOUISIANA

Top: The Diamond Horseshoe Truck Stop (T-118) was a Second Generation truck stop operated by Oliver Wolfe in this circa-1964 photo, and was located on U.S. Highway 20 outside of S. Sioux City, Nebraska. This busy establishment sports a giant "Diamond Horseshoe Restaurant" neon signage atop the restaurant, at left, with "Chicken, Steaks, Bar & Grill" neon to the right (odd, considering that, in order to be a truck stop in the Skelly Truck Stop network, the proprietor must refrain from selling intoxicating beverages). "Skelly Super Service" neon is on the rooftop just above the late-1950s Chevy and Ford autos. Horizontal neon runs the length of the restaurant building fasçia, from around the corner at left, to the single diesel service bay at right. Restaurant, showers, and 24-hour service are mentioned in the 1963 Skelly Truck Stop Directory, but sleeping facilities are not, thus qualifying this location to be only a Fuel Stop, by Skelly's own corporate-mandated standards. The fuel pump islands, sporting six 1950s-era globe-topped pumps, sit on a concrete slab, surrounded by gravel approaches.

Bottom: This Crystal Oil Co. truck stop (T-117), located on U.S. Highway 77 in South Sioux City, Nebraska, was operated by John Hickey, and featured an elaborate roadside neon sign as one of its most prominent features in this circa-1965 photo: "Crystal" is spelled out in diamonds across the top, with neon tracer-light arrows surrounding "Café" on the roadside and bottom sides; "Truckers Lodge" is spelled out beneath. The Crystal Café is at left, with the fuel office at center, and the showers and sleeping facilities to the right of that. "Crystal Oil Co." is spelled out in neon across the roofline. The fuel pumps are of the early-1960s variety, sans globes.

An early Third Generation truck stop, Calhoun, Louisiana's Pelican I-20 Truck Stop (T-158) was built in the early 1960s, and was operated by Clinton Harp at that time; William P. Heard was the operator by the mid-1960s. By 1968, Lee Petroleum Co., Inc. was listed as the operator, and by 1978, J. D. Peters was operating this facility. By 1980, Judge C. Duchesne was operating the now re-named Judge Truck Stop. From a high of approximately 10 Skelly branded Truck Stops and Fuel Stops operating in Louisiana in the mid-1960s, the Getty takeover of Skelly in the early 1980s reduced the number to zero. The 1963 list of amenities for this truck stop include, "Recreation Hall, Pool Table, Lubridome, and Cattle Motel (Capacity 10 Loads)." The roadside neon advertising, "Repair Services," "Bunks," and "TWX" (wire services) eclipses the plastic backlit Skelly sign by nearly a factor of two. It appears that graveled-dirt approaches and exits were still the norm at this point. A GMC DF-series "Crackerbox" cabover tractor-trailer sits perpendicular to the fuel island.

In the early 1960s, the 3 & 71 Truck Stop (T-190), located at the intersection of State Highway 3 and U.S. Highway 71, nine miles north of Storm Lake, Iowa, was just a line drawing on a drawing board. By 1963, operators George Saunders and Ken Jorgensen were operating this modern, attractive early Third Generation truck stop/motel complex; Howard Sabel came on board as an additional operator in 1968. In about 1976, Bob Lyman was listed as the Manager. There is nothing to indicate that this outlet was still operating as a Skelly or Getty branded truck stop by 1984. While the entire lot of the truck stop appears to be paved in asphalt and concrete, the Crossroads Motel lot appears to be graveled, except for the parking area immediately adjacent to the motel rooms. In 1970, "Separate showers for ladies" had been added.

HOLGER ANDERSON'S TRUCK STOP
ON U. S. 77 AND ST. 38A — I 90, 3 BLKS., N., I 29, 3 MI. W.
SIOUX FALLS, SO. DAKOTA

TRUCK HARBOR
STATE HIGHWAY No. 13 — 5½ Miles South Of
BOLIVAR, MISSOURI

Before a large-scale revamp in the late 1950s or early '60s, Holger Anderson's truck stop was known in the '40s as, "Anderson's Super Multiple Pump Station and Café." Anderson's Skelly Truck Stop (T-148) dates to at least the early 1960s as a Skelly branded establishment. An expansive complex, this truck stop was located at the junction of I-90, U.S. Highway 77, and Highway 38A in Sioux Falls, South Dakota. It is cutting edge Second Generation in this iteration: the sizeable lot is fully-paved (with the exception of the graveled entrances) and Skelly backlit plastic road signs face all lanes of the intersection. The pump island office is located at center, with a three-bay service building to its right. The second-floor sleeping dorm can be seen to the left of the fuel office; one of the two buildings further left likely houses the café, showers, and/or perhaps the listed "lounge room and meeting rooms." Robert Eleeson is listed as a Manager by 1964; Harlan Wehde replaces Eleeson in 1970, with Leonard Wittrock succeeding Mr. Wehde in 1976. Lawerence Anderson was operating the Getty branded Fuel Stop by 1984.

Grover Stottlemyre was operating Bolivar, Missouri's Truck Harbor (T-128) by at least as early as 1963. Located on Missouri State Highway 13, 5.5 miles south of Bolivar, this low-slung, ranch house-style operation with the large neon TRUCK HARBOR signage across the roofline featured "Bunks," according to the Skelly pole sign at roadside; by about 1966, a "12 Unit Motel" upgraded the bunks at this facility. The KB Series International wrecker at left was a style introduced in 1947; the International pickup truck at right was introduced about 10 years later. There's a 1963 Chevy truck fueling just right of center, and a 1958 Chevy auto fueling closest to the building. In about 1978, Norman J. Weddell had assumed the management responsibilities. This photo was used to illustrate this truck stop in the Skelly Truck Stop Directories as late as the 1980 edition, despite the outdated gravel lot and ancient vehicles. This outlet apparently did not make the cut with Getty in the early-1980s Skelly-to-Getty conversion.

GRIMM OIL CO. TRUCK STOP
INTERSTATE 74 AND NORTH MORTON AVE.
THE TRUCK STOP THAT "HAS EVERYTHING"
MORTON, ILLINOIS

In 1966, Ray Wilhelm's Marshall Truck Stop (T-213), located on U.S. Highway 77, five miles north of Beatrice, Nebraska, opened its doors. This tidy little facility sported an all-gravel lot and parking area, and six pumps on two concrete islands. Rod Marshall (owner) was operating this outlet by 1970; by the time of the Skelly-to-Getty conversion, Mr. Marshall had assigned operational duties to Manager Paul Perry. A circa-1964 Pontiac can be seen fueling.

"The Truck Stop That Has Everything" was the slogan for Dan E. Grimm's Grimm Oil Co. Truck Stop (T-160), located at I-74 and N. Morton Ave. in Morton, Illinois. Who could disregard that huge red neon command to EAT adorning the second floor sleeping rooms? By 1980, that huge EAT sign had been moved to the left, atop a hideous mansard-roofed second floor addition over the restaurant with which 1976 operator Dan R. Grimm had assaulted the original architecture. The early 1980s conversion from Skelly to Getty saw this outlet being dropped by Getty. Early 1960s Mack conventional and early 3000 Series White cabover trucks can be seen fueling at far right.

HILLTOP SKELLY TRUCK STOP
U. S. 69, 2 MILES NORTH, ROUTE 3
Complete Friendly Service
MUSKOGEE, OKLAHOMA

Two miles north of Muskogee, Oklahoma, on U.S. Highway 69 near the intersection of U.S. Highway 62 (Route #3), owner D. C. Hilton and lessee Glenn Smith operated the Hilltop Skelly Truck Stop (T-166). This pre-1963 photo shows various sizes of truck tires for sale in front of the sleeping facility at left (Truckers Motel), and the giant "Hilltop Truck-O-Tel" signage on the second floor of the main building. Of the 12 fuel pumps visible in the photo, 10 are of 1960s manufacture; two near center (a red one and a green one) are of 1950s-vintage and feature pump-top globes. At right, a late 1960s White conventional and an early '60s B-Model Mack conventional are parked together; further right, a mid-'50s Kenworth cabover sits alone. Charles Kennedy had assumed control of this outlet by 1976, and Don Walden was at the controls when it became rebranded to Getty in the early 1980s.

Some of the largest signs ever developed for the petroleum industry were the huge Skelly truck stop signs. With signs as large as sixteen feet square, mounted on poles that were as high as 110 feet, these signs were welcoming beacons that could be seen for miles. This example was photographed in 1985 at the Grimm Oil Company truck stop in Morton, Illinois.

A late-1950s Hendrickson conventional fuels at a Kaw Valley, Kansas, stockyard Skelly facility. The exact location is unknown.

SOHIO and Affiliates

Standard Oil Co. of Ohio

• Founded in 1870 by John D. Rockefeller, Standard Oil Co. of Ohio is the direct descendant of the original Standard Oil.

• Assigned only refining and marketing in Ohio with the 1911 breakup of Standard Oil.

• Began building a retail chain of service stations by 1915.

• Introduced the SOHIO brand name in 1928 for their premium grade of gasoline. Began using SOHIO as its primary brand name in 1930.

• Purchased the Fleetwing gasoline marketing operations of the Spears and Riddle Co. in 1928, and offered the Fleetwing name to independent jobbers in Ohio and surrounding states. The balance of the Fleetwing operation, found in much of the eastern U.S. was sold off or abandoned at that time.

• SOHIO purchased a minority interest in Canfield Oil Co. in 1929. SOHIO would complete the purchase in 1945 and eventually rebrand the Canfield operations to SOHIO.

• SOHIO introduced a new gasoline in 1954 with the chemical Boron as an additive. This product proved so successful that the process would be licensed to other marketers, including DX and Richfield Oil Co. of California.

• In 1956 SOHIO opened their first company-owned gas station outside of Ohio, at Covington, Kentucky. This station, prohibited from using the SOHIO name due to agreements that traced back to the breakup of Standard Oil, would be branded after the company's new premium grade gasoline, Boron. During the 1960s, other Boron branded gas stations would be built in Pennsylvania and Michigan.

• In the late 1960s, SOHIO became involved in a complex transaction with British Petroleum (BP), which eventually led to SOHIO trading control of the company to BP in exchange for access to Alaska crude oil fields that were currently being developed by BP. SOHIO would eventually become known as BP America in the 1980s.

• Almost all usage of the SOHIO name would be phased-out in 1990 in favor of the BP brand name.

• See the BP section for more information

Truck Stop Operations

• SOHIO's distribution network had locally-supplied several truck stops in Ohio as early as the 1930s.

Parks-Klay Co., local Fleet Wing jobber, operated the P-K Truck Stop, located at the intersection of U.S. 30 and U.S. 25 in Beaverdam, Ohio. This location is an example of where a roadside farmhouse was converted to a restaurant and then expanded into a full truck stop operation. It is shown here in a 1950 photo.

The Shenandoah Inn was a SOHIO branded truck stop facility on Interstate 70 at Old Washington, Ohio. As SOHIO's truck stop network evolved in the 1960s, the facilities became more elaborate. This is an example of a truck stop that also included a full motel, a gift shop and a truckers' store, in addition to the usual restaurant and fuel sales. This photo dates from about 1975.

This is the oldest example we have of a truck stop selling SOHIO products. Smitty's Truck Stop was located on U.S. 22 and Ohio Route 3-C, about 18 miles northeast of Cincinnati. A 24-hour restaurant and ample truck parking were among the amenities offered. This photo dates from about 1950.

Typical of the 1960s SOHIO truck stop network, Stop 127 was located on Interstate 70 at U.S. 127, in Eaton, Ohio. These photographs date from about 1970.

• In 1963, SOHIO began the formal development of a truck stop network along Interstate highways in Ohio. This was later expanded into other states under the Boron brand.

• In 1987, BP purchased Truckstops of America. Some T/A locations began selling products under the Boron brand.

• SOHIO and Boron truck stops were rebranded to BP, with the finalizing of the brand consolidation in 1989 and 1990.

Fleetwing Corp.

• Fleetwing traces its roots to the 1870s, in Wheeling, West Virginia.

• Purchased by SOHIO in the late 1920s; the Fleetwing brand name was then offered to marketers in Ohio and surrounding states who purchased petroleum products from them.

• SOHIO later moved Fleetwing's corporate headquarters to Cleveland, Ohio, and established the Fleetwing Corp. as a brand for independent jobbers in Pennsylvania, West Virginia, Michigan, and Ohio.

• Fleetwing was purchased by Pennzoil in about 1968.

• *Number of confirmed Fleetwing branded truck stops operating in the U.S.:* As many as a dozen Fleetwing locations are known to have been jobber- or dealer-operated truck stops.

Another of SOHIO's ever-expanding network of truck stops was Stop 35, on Interstate 71 at U.S. 35, south of Columbus, Ohio. Diesel fuel facilities were located in the rear, with a complete SOHIO service station in the front. A restaurant, truckers' store, and repair facilities occupy the large building in the center of the complex. These photos date from about 1970.

Stony Creek Truck Terminal

Take a good location, such as this one on U.S. 301 at Stony Creek, Virginia, add a good restaurant, lots of parking, Blue SUNOCO gasoline, and a bunkhouse out back, and you had what passed for a truck stop in the 1940s.

SUNOCO

SUNOCO Refining & Marketing Co.

• Founded in 1890 by Joseph Newton Pew and family from holdings purchased from a natural gas producer who had purchased several oil leases in the Lima, Ohio, area in 1886.

• Entered retail gasoline marketing in 1920. By 1930, marketing could be found from Maine to Virginia and in Florida. No effort was made to connect the northern markets with Florida until the company began expansion in 1956.

• Merged with Sunray DX Oil Company (DX) in 1968. By 1971 the combined company was marketing under the SUNOCO brand east of the Mississippi River, and under DX brand in the mid-continent area.

• Representation remained relatively thin in the Carolinas and Georgia, and the company began to withdraw from some markets in 1984.

• Acquired the reborn Atlantic Refining Co. in 1988. Atlantic gas stations in Pennsylvania and New York were rebranded to SUNOCO in the 1990s.

• In recent years, SUNOCO has begun rebuilding its exposure, primarily through jobbers, in Virginia and the Carolinas.

Truck Stop Operations

• SUNOCO made no particular effort to enter the truck stop market. However, it is known that at least one SUNOCO truck stop, a dealer-owned site, was operating by the late 1940s in Virginia.

• *Number of confirmed SUNOCO branded truck stops operating in the U.S.:* A late 1960s SUNOCO inventory confirms 123 sites in 17 states pumping diesel fuel, although none are clearly defined as being a "truck stop."

• Confirmed SUNOCO branded truck stop totals range from as few as one in 1970 to as many as 23 in 1984, with most intervening years confirming a dozen or so.

TENNECO and Affiliates

Bay Petroleum Co., later TENNECO Oil Co.

• Founded in MacPherson, Kansas, in 1935.

• Most Bay stations were rebranded to TENNECO in about 1961 following the purchase of the company by the Tennessee Gas Transmission Co.

• When TENNECO decided to get out of direct gasoline marketing in about 1988, many Georgia and Florida Bay stations were sold to Tifton, Georgia's Dixie Oil Co.

• A handful of Bay outlets operated into the late 1990s, although none as truck stops.

• The Bay logo, last revised in 1939, is the most resilient oil company logo, having survived, without revision, to ever be associated with a U.S. oil company.

Truck Stop Operations

• *Number of confirmed Bay branded truck stops operating in the U.S.:*

• Bay branded several truck stop locations in the Midwest prior to their association with TENNECO.

• Several former Citizens and Speed branded locations in the southeastern U.S. were operating as truck stops when the parent company was purchased by Bay. Bay continued to operated them as truck stops, but never presented them as a "network."

• After many Bay locations were rebranded to TENNECO, some of the truck stops may have also carried the TENNECO brand. Use of the TENNECO name, which began in 1962, was spotty and many locations had reverted to the Bay brand after a few years.

• TENNECO operated a truck stop at Ennis, Texas, that carried their Direct brand.

Bair's was a chain of truck stops that operated throughout the northern Rocky Mountain area, with sites offering Bay brand petroleum products. The original Bair's sites, such as this one on U.S. 10 in Bozeman, Montana, incorporated some elements of Bay's standard station design into their architecture, including the central pylon with Bay lettering. After TENNECO purchased Bay and rebranded the operation, much of the Bay marketing in the Rockies was sold to FINA. This photo dates from about 1962.

This might be one of the more interesting truck stop configurations we've seen. The Havana Truck Terminal was located on U.S. 27 in Havana, Florida, and sold fuels under the Citizens 77 brand. The small station office had been supplemented by a large truck service bay in the rear, with rooms upstairs of the bay, accessed by an outside stairway. A diner and an ice plant were also located on the site. It is shown here in about 1958.

Another Bair's truck stop was located in West Yellowstone, Montana, this one decidedly aimed more at tourists than truckers. A 40-room motel was included in addition to food and fuel. By the time this photo was taken in the late 1960s, the FINA brand had replaced the Bay brand at Bair's stops.

TEXACO

- Founded in Port Arthur, Texas (near Beaumont), in 1902 by "Buckskin Joe" Cullinan and Arnold Schlaet.
- TEXACO was the first U.S. oil company to operate retail marketing in all states (1928), and in all 50 states by the 1960s.
- TEXACO's famous "Havoline" brand of engine oils and lubricants was originally the property of the Indian Refining Company. Indian Refining Co. was founded on March 16, 1911. TEXACO purchased Indian Refining in 1931 primarily for their Havoline lubricants production capacity and brand recognition. TEXACO continued to use the trademarked Indian Gas brand name for their motor grade gasoline until after WWII.
- TEXACO survived with their national marketing intact through the gas shortages of the 1970s, however litigation from Pennzoil after the Getty purchase forced TEXACO to near bankruptcy, and a forced scale-back of all retail operations.
- Control of the TEXACO brand passed, in part, to Shell in the late 1990s, who nearly eliminated the brand, and later to Chevron, who is currently striving to re-establish it.

Truck Stop Operations

- Being a national marketer, the TEXACO brand appeared on numerous truck stops from the 1930s forward. However, there was no great effort to organize TEXACO's truck stops until the 1960s.
- Varying standards for truck stops and varying methods of data collection make it difficult to determine an accurate count of TEXACO truck stops before about 1970.
- TEXACO purchased the Getty Oil Company in the mid-1980s, and through the acquisition of Getty's Skelly truck stop network, became the world leader in the number of branded truck stops.
- *Number of confirmed TEXACO branded truck stops operating in the U.S. by year:*

1966: 403
1969: 351
1972: 118
1975: 139
1977: 137
1979: 130
1981: 125
1984: 143
1991: 366

Tower TEXACO Truck Stop was built in the early 1960s in Tower City, North Dakota, and was one of the first truck stops to operate along the newly completed stretch of Interstate 94 that ran through town. Features included a large coffee shop and restaurant, truck service bays and tire service, and two grades of TEXACO diesel fuel, both the premium grade Diesel Chief, and the regular grade #2 diesel. It is shown here in about 1964.

Strategic points along highways were prime locations for truck stops. On Virginia's eastern shore, U.S. 13 was originally funneled onto a ferry at Cape Charles, and in 1952, the ferry landing shifted south to Kiptopeke, Virginia. The Cape Center restaurant and truck stop was located along U.S. 13 between Cape Charles and Kiptopeke, and served as a "last stop" before the crossing. In 1964, the Chesapeake Bay Bridge and Tunnel opened just south of Kiptopeke, and Cape Center continued to serve truckers and motorists. By the 1960s it had rebranded to PURE and was in PURE's truck stop program. Today it is an EXXON branded Convenience Store. It is shown here in about 1956.

Advertised as a one-stop station for truckers, tourists, and locals, Harmon's TEXACO Truck Stop and 2-87 Diner was located at the intersection of U.S. 2 and U.S. 87 in Havre, Montana. One large building included the restaurant, a truckers' store, and complete truck service. Eleven pumps dispensed TEXACO products; parking, though still a graveled lot, encompassed six acres. This classic truck stop was photographed here in about 1960.

Olde Fort Truck Stop included a 1960s then-modern steel building that housed the restaurant and fuel desk. Located on U.S. 31W just two miles north of Bowling Green, Kentucky, they advertised three acres of parking, truck repair and tire service, individual sleeping rooms, and a complete restaurant. It is seen here in about 1965.

Crown Point Motor Park opened on U.S. 130 in Thorofare, New Jersey, in 1936, making it one of the earliest truck stops in the country. Truck service was their specialty, servicing all makes, while maintaining an International Trucks sales agency. TEXACO products were sold here, as well, when the facility was photographed in 1964.

Another predecessor to today's travel stops were the themed stops of the 1960s. Hillbilly Junction was one such stop. Located on U.S. 60-63 in Willow Springs, Missouri, Hillbilly Junction was thematically similar to today's Cracker Barrel locations. This photo is from about 1970.

Pete's Truck Stop in Sioux Falls, South Dakota, made advantageous use of signage. In addition to the TEXACO signage advertising fuel, a large neon signboard with a red "Truck Stop" arrow pointed the way to the facility, while the restaurant and other features were listed below. Propane for refrigeration units was dispensed right on the fuel island, and three large service bays were ready for truck service. It is shown here in about 1960.

The Roadrunner Truck Stop was located in Phoenix, Arizona, and was a prototype for today's travel plazas. Canopied fuel islands provided shade from Arizona's year-round radiant sunshine; a restaurant, a truckers' store, and a motel (complete with pool!) was located at the rear of the lot. Signage indicates specific auto or truck fueling positions. It is seen here as it appeared in 1962.

The Nebo Truck Stop is located along Interstate 40 at the exit for Nebo, North Carolina. Built during the early 1960s, it was at the time a minimum service facility featuring only an eatery and two brands of fuel (TEXACO and American). It continues to operate today, although the TEXACO building has been enlarged into a modern Convenience Store. It is shown here about 1965.

Advertised at the first truck stop in Florida, Butler's Truck Stop was located on U.S. 1-301 north of Jacksonville, Florida, and is believed to have been opened in the late 1930s. In this era, the facilities were limited to simply a full service restaurant and TEXACO fueling facilities. A second Butler's truck stop was later located outside of Jacksonville on U.S. 17 and Florida Highway A1A. The original location is shown here in about 1950.

Construction on the Ohio Turnpike began in 1949, with portions of the road opening in 1954 and the balance in 1955. Service plazas are located along the highway, as is the norm on most toll roads. During the 1960s, TEXACO was a concessionaire at some of the service plazas, which functioned as truck stops along the Turnpike. Shown here is one of the facilities as it appeared with TEXACO branding.

Mid Way Truck Stop was located on U.S. 301-52 just south of Florence, South Carolina. A modern diner for the era, and TEXACO fuels were just two of the amenities available here. This photograph dates from 1958.

J. W. Lyles operated the Transitruck Center in Laurel, Maryland, from the late 1940s through the 1970s, along with another truck stop at Millersville, Maryland. The Transitruck is an example of the classic truck stop found on the East Coast. The large building at center housed the restaurant and fuel service desk, along with a truckers' store, while upstairs bunkrooms for drivers could be found. Widely spaced fuel islands and scales occupied the front of the lot, while services such as ice for truck refrigeration was handled in a separate building. It is seen here in about 1955.

Union Oil Co.

UNION 76/UNOCAL 76/National Access 76, et al.

• UNION 76 was founded in 1890 in Santa Paula, California, by Lyman Stewart, who merged several small predecessor holdings.

• Began retail marketing of gasoline in 1913, and by 1940, was marketing in California, Oregon, Washington, Nevada, and Idaho.

• UNION purchased the PURE Oil Co. in 1965, and in 1968 began a gradual rebranding of the PURE marketing to the UNION 76 brand. With the completion of this effort in 1970, UNION Oil was in retail gasoline marketing coast-to-coast.

• Renamed UNOCAL Corp. in 1983, in 1985, UNOCAL's primary brand became "UNOCAL 76."

• During the late 1980s, UNOCAL marketing in some states in the upper Midwest was sold to a joint venture between UNOCAL and the Venezuelan state oil company known as Uno-Ven.

• In 1991, it was announced that UNOCAL would withdraw from marketing in the southeastern U.S. UNOCAL jobbers formed a co-operative and licensed the PURE brand from UNOCAL. This co-operative remains in operation today and the PURE brand can again be found throughout the southeastern U.S.

• In 1997, UNOCAL sold off their "76" brand and the remaining portions of their marketing operations to Tosco. Tosco was sold to Phillips Petroleum in 2001, and Phillips merged with CONOCO in 2002. Today CONOCOPhillips markets under the 76 brand on the West Coast.

Truck Stop Operations

• In the early 1960s, UNION Oil began opening truck stops in conjunction with key bulk plants and terminals throughout its marketing area. Unique to the industry, these truck stops consisted of unattended dispensing equipment controlled by coded key systems. This was the extent of Union's truck stop marketing prior to the purchase of PURE, and might logically be considered to be the forerunner of today's "pumper" truck stops.

• After completion of the PURE-UNION 76 rebranding, UNION Oil continued to operate the truck stop network in much the same way that PURE had. New sites were added, and sites that no longer met the ever-increasing standards for truck stops were

The typical UNION 76 truck stop of the 1970s and 1980s was a refinement of designs initiated by the PURE Oil Co. in the 1960s. The St. Louis East Truck Plaza in Troy, Illinois, was no exception. A large central building housed restaurant, store, lounge, and service facilities; canopied fueling positions extended from the building. Typical of Third Generation truck stops, separate entrances are marked for cars and trucks. This photo shows the location as it appeared in about 1980.

Kelly's Truck Terminal is another example of how UNION Oil refined the PURE truck stop formatting concepts. A massive canopy structure extends from the building out over the truck fueling islands, while smaller canopies cover auto gas islands in the front. Kelly's was located on U.S. 79-80, where the highway crosses Interstate 20 outside of Shreveport, Louisiana, and is shown here in about 1980.

dropped from the program.

• By 1976, UNION 76 owned approximately 315 Auto/Truck Centers. These included 278 PURE branded truck stops purchased in 1965 and 37 UNION 76 branded truck stops and fuel stops in the western U.S.

• The 1976 "UNION 76 National TruckStop Directory" delineated between its "Auto/TruckStops" ("Has separate islands to serve passenger cars") and its "TruckStops" ("Does not have a separate passenger car island"). By 1978, the "UNION 76 National TruckStop Directory" softened the wording in the "TruckStops" listings to stress that its truck stops "…*may* not have separate passenger car island."

• The 1988 UNOCAL 76 National Auto/TruckStop Directory prefaced its "separate passenger car island" listings with, "Denotes TruckStop locations off the Interstates."

• By 1990, the UNOCAL 76 National Auto/Truck-Stop Directory, 100th Anniversary Edition, separated their trucking-related outlets into three categories: Auto/TruckStops (…all open 24 hours, 365 days a year, and have separate truck and passenger car fuel islands; …all are located on the Interstates or major expressways); Fuel Stops (Many are interstate locations with full facilities and have separate truck fuel islands); and Diesel Stops (on major highways and generally are not open 24 hours). This is the point where the 76 brand completes the transition from "truck stops" to the auto-based "travel plaza."

• The corporate name was changed to UNOCAL 76 in 1985.

• UNOCAL retreated from the truck stop business in 1993, selling all truck stop holdings to National Auto/Truckstops (National Access); in 1997 National Auto/Truckstops ceased to exist when TravelCenters of America (T/A) purchased all 122 locations.

• *Number of confirmed 76 branded truck stops operating in the U.S. by year:*

1966: 37
1967: 18
1968: 13
1969: 232 (Acquisition of PURE's truck stop network)
1972: 320
1975: 310
1976: 333
1978: 309
1981: 281
1983: 272
1984: 232
1985: 258
1988: 247
1990: 195
1991: 209
1993: 141

Corbin, Kentucky, was a major highway junction for most of the twentieth century; a location where divergent branches of U.S. 25 re-converged. It was also home to a mid-century burgeoning fried chicken restaurant entrepreneur named Harland Sanders. Sanders operated "Sanders Court & Café," a tourist court operation that also housed a PURE gas station. In 1952, Sanders sold the recipe for his delectable fried chicken to a gentleman named Pete Harman who was operating a restaurant in Salt Lake City, Utah, and "Colonel" Sander's Kentucky Fried Chicken empire was born. In later years, Interstate 75 bypassed Corbin, giving Sanders the idea to franchise his chicken recipe nationwide. This bypass of Corbin created ideal locations for truck stops along the new north-south corridor. The original King's Truck Town first appears in PURE truck stop directories in 1964, when the operation was located on U.S. 25 north. When the PURE brand was replaced by UNION 76 in 1970, the relocated facility was rebranded to UNION 76. Today the location is known as the Corbin Travel Plaza, and Marathon petroleum products are sold.

An interesting combination of names: The C and C Truck Stop located just off of Interstate 35 at Olathe, Kansas, also included the B and B Café. Vickers products were sold here and were advertised with the classic "gas for less" appellation. It is shown here in about 1960.

Valero and Affiliates (Beacon & Shamrock & Total Affiliates)

• Valero was founded in 1980 and originally operated as a natural gas producer and distributor, and is a consolidation of a number of independent refiner/marketers located all across the U.S.

There are two major components that comprise Valero:

1—Ultramar Diamond Shamrock, the result of a merger of Ultramar and its California operations (specifically Beacon Oil, purchased in 1981), with Texas-based Diamond Shamrock. Ultramar and Diamond Shamrock had merged in 1996.

2—Total Petroleum, a unit of the French-based Total Oil Co., that entered U.S. markets with the 1970 purchase of Michigan's Leonard Refineries. (Additional Total acquisitions include Anderson Prichard Oil in 1978, and Vickers Petroleum in 1980.)

• Ultramar Diamond Shamrock and Total Petroleum merged in 1997. In 2000, the Valero brand was introduced to consolidate all of the company's marketing under a single brand. After it had been considered that some secondary locations existed, both the Shamrock and the Beacon names have been preserved for possible current or later usage.

Leonard Oil Co. identified itself with Michigan's outdoor sportsmen, and sought out locations where its fuel products would be marketed in lodges and other locations that appealed to hunters, fishermen, and others who participated in outdoor activities. Ruth's Lunch Room was one such location, but by virtue of its location on U.S. 16 west of Lansing, served as a convenient stop for truckers traveling the highway, as well. It is seen here in about 1958.

Beacon Oil Co.

• Founded by Walter Allen and a four associates in 1931 as The Caminol Co. At that time it was operating a small refinery in the Los Angeles area, and less than a dozen gas stations, under the "Beacon" and "Kettleman" brand names.

• After a second refinery was obtained in Hanford in about 1967, the name was changed to Beacon.

• At the peak of the operation, Beacon operated nearly 300 gas stations in the early 1980s.

• During the early 1980s, Beacon also operated "Bingo Fuel Systems, Inc." as a secondary gas station brand, with outlets located in Arizona, California, Idaho, Illinois, Iowa, Kansas, Missouri, Nebraska, Nevada, New Mexico, Oklahoma, Oregon, South Dakota, Texas, Utah, Washington, and Wyoming. Diesel fuel was sold at some Bingo locations, but there were no Bingo branded truck stops.

• Beacon was acquired by Ultramar (currently Ultramar Diamond Shamrock) in 1981. After having merged with Total Petroleum's United States operations, the surviving company operates today as Valero.

• *Number of confirmed Beacon branded truck stops operating in the U.S.:* Approximately 18 Beacon branded truck stops operated between 1970 and 1984 in California, Arizona, Nevada, and New Mexico.

Shamrock Oil & Gas Co.

• Founded on August, 09, 1929 in Amarillo, Texas.

• Shamrock merged with Diamond Alkalai Co. in 1967 to become Diamond Shamrock. In 1996, Diamond Shamrock later merged with Canada's Ultramar Oil Co. to form Ultramar Diamond Shamrock.

• *Number of confirmed Shamrock branded truck stops operating in the U.S. by year:*

1969: As many as 171 "truck stops" were confirmed, although most of these outlets were simply gas stations that also operated a diesel pump. Many were listed as having a café or sleeping facilities "nearby."
1970: 13
1971: 16
1975: 17
1976: 11
1977: 17
1979: 15
1981: 12
1984: 26 (Many may have been cross-branded by this time)
1995: 2

Shamrock Oil Company marketed throughout a thinly populated area in western Texas, New Mexico, and into surrounding states. At strategic locations throughout their territory they began locating truck stops and encouraging their dealers and marketers to do the same. This example, at an unknown location, shows one of the designs developed during the early 1960s.

In this photo, taken by a trucker in the late 1950s, we see a rural truck stop selling Shamrock products. It was likely located in western Texas.

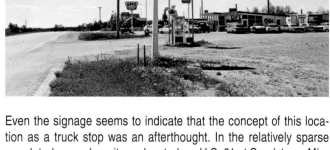

Even the signage seems to indicate that the concept of this location as a truck stop was an afterthought. In the relatively sparse populated area where it was located, on U.S. 61 at Sandstone, Minnesota, the facility served an important need, however. With APCO gasoline and diesel fuel, and an attached café, they catered to the north-south truck traffic in the area. It is seen here about 1960.

Anderson Prichard Oil Co. (APCO)

• Founded in Oklahoma City in 1921. Marketed Col-Tex products in several midwestern states prior to 1930.

• In 1946, Col-Tex stations in Oklahoma were rebranded to APCO, while other marketing territories continued to use Col-Tex.

• In 1952, APCO purchased Kanotex and rebranded all Kanotex and Anderson-Prichard outlets to APCO. Col-Tex was sold to the Cosden Oil Co. of Big Spring, Texas, a firm that operated gas stations in about six states, but no truck stops.

• APCO was purchased by Ashland Oil Co. of Ashland, Kentucky, in the late 1950s.

• France's Total Petroleum purchased APCO from Ashland in 1978. Total began rebranding all APCO outlets to Total in the 1990s.

• *Number of confirmed APCO branded truck stops operating in the U.S.:* Fewer than a half-dozen APCO branded truck stops have been confirmed, all having operated between 1970 and 1984. These locations were operated by or in conjunction with APCO's jobber network.

Independent Brands

Virtually *every* regional petroleum marketer in the U.S. can claim there having been one or more "truck stops" (considering a loose interpretation of the term) operated under their corporate brand, at one time or another, many via "Mom & Pop"-type truck stops. Excluding those listed above, these would include, but are not necessarily limited to: Agway, APEX, Arrow, Astro, Bell, Best, Bi-Lo, Bingo, BI-RITE, Buzz, CENEX, Cirillo Bros., Clark, CO-OP, Crown, Crystal, Crystal Flash, Del-Tex, Derby, Douglas, E-Qual, FuelEx, Fuel Mart, Gas Bar, Giant, Gladieux, GoMart, GoCo, Hancock, Herman, Hess, Hubbard, Imperial, Key, Keystone, Knox, Klepper, Kwik-Fill, Lion, Malco, Marine, Mars, Martin, Mohawk, Morgan, National, Olympic, Pacer, Pennzoil, Plateau, Premier, Platolene, Premium, Quaker State, Quality Gas, RaceTrac, Red Ace, Seago, Silco, Sioux, SipCo, S.O.C., Spur, Sunland, SuperPar, SuperTest, Tesoro, Texgas, Travel Port, Trico, Truck Terminal Motels, Trucker's World, Tulsa, TruckOMat, Ultramar, United, U.S. Pumper, U.S. Service, Vickers, Webbco, WECO, Welco, Westland, White Rose, Whiting Bros., Wings, and Zephyr.

The Bluebird Truck Stop was one of the most complete truck stops in the South. Founded by Clyde and Frank Bartlett in 1939, it was still operating as late as 1994. The Bluebird was located at Pryor St. and Memorial Dr. in Atlanta, Georgia, just off Interstates 20, 75 and 85. The facility served as a major truck service center and as a distributor for Cooper Tires and Chevron RPM motor oils. It is seen here in about 1970.

Shortly after WWII, Crown Central Petroleum began searching out existing facilities for distribution of Crown products. Truckers Terminal on North Tryon St. in Charlotte was one of the first locations to offer Crown products in North Carolina. At the time this photo was taken in 1951, the facility featured air-conditioned bunk rooms, a diner, and a dispatch service. This location was later rebranded to a PURE truck stop.

Even relatively obscure private brand operations had at least one location they considered to be a truck stop. Anchor Oil operated the T and M Truck Stop on U.S. 441 just south of Okeechobee, Florida. On premises was a diner, and facilities that included a truckers' lounge and TV room, and a bunkhouse. It is seen here in about 1965.

The U.S. 21 Truck Stop was located, logically, on U.S. 21 between Rock Hill, South Carolina, and Charlotte, North Carolina. Built in the early 1950s using the twin pylon design developed by Crown Central Petroleum, the facility featured two additional oversized service bays for truck service and an attached restaurant. In later years this facility, too, became a PURE truck stop.

In early 1963, the latest incarnation of "The World's Largest Service Station," a Derby branded truck stop, opened on Interstate 35 just north of Oklahoma City, Oklahoma. Truckers Village was a joint venture between experienced truck stop operator Richard Keele and Derby jobber Wendell Sandlin. The facility opened with 57 pumps on a five-acre lot, surpassing the previous "largest" gas station (Little America) by two pumps. Signage included a full size tractor trailer mounted on a pedestal with neon lettering covering the trailer. Features of the stop included ten bunk rooms, a TV lounge, showers, on-site laundromat, 24-hour truck service, and an automatic truck wash. It is seen here at the time it opened in 1963.

Deem Oil Company developed a chain of nearly 60 service stations in the St. Louis, Missouri area. In the spring of 1958 Derby Oil purchased the operation and rebranded the network to Derby. Shown here is Deem's flagship station and truck stop, shortly after conversion to the Derby brand.

The El Paso brand was introduced when El Paso Natural Gas purchased McNutt Oil Co. and its extensive station network. McNutt had been a member of Dixie Distributors, resulting in dual-branded El Paso/Dixie sites. In this shot, we see Miller's Truck City, a full service truck stop at Kingman, Arizona, in about 1960.

The Border El Paso Dixie Truck Terminal was a rare example of an in-town truck stop. Located at 3700 E. Paisano Drive in El Paso, they catered both to trucks serving the border area and tourists that frequently visited. Advertisements indicate that restaurants and motels were nearby. We see it here as it appeared in 1959.

Another example of a strategically located service station making itself over into a truck stop. Dunlap's Service was located at the west end of Willcox, Arizona, and offered 24-hour service, tire repair, and an on-site café. It is seen here as it appeared in 1954.

As fuel prices increased after the first gas shortage of the 1970s, some truck stop operators eliminated services in favor of "price marketing," attracting business with deeply discounted fuel prices. Farris Oil Co. was one such operator, with this location at Wells, Nevada. Included was an early version of today's Convenience Store.

Grant's Truck and Car Stops were founded in Boise, Idaho, and date to at least the late 1940s. David Grant's original site, shown here, was located on U.S. 20-26-30 just east of Boise, and is shown here in about 1955 in the daytime scene, and a decade later in the night shot. Other locations were opened in York, Nebraska, and Lupton, Arizona.

After Interstate 80 was built through Boise, Grants relocated its facilities to a new location at the Broadway exit. The new location featured truck repair facilities and a much larger restaurant. It is seen here in the late 1960s.

Foote Oil Co. operated this truck stop on U.S. 30 east of Kearney, Nebraska. Complete truck service and free showers were advertised amenities. It is shown here as it existed in about 1965.

The Moasis Truck-O-Tel and Restaurant was an early combination stop that advertised itself to truckers and tourists alike. It was located on U.S. 41 at Little Chute, Wisconsin. This photo is from about 1970.

The Famous Service Truck Stop was located at the Napier exit off Interstate 94 in Benton Harbor, Michigan. Even as late at the early 1960s date of this photo the facility included a large graveled lot.

The Mountain View Truck Stop, located on U.S. 601, approximately six miles south of Monroe, North Carolina, was operated by the Helms family. In addition to the usual food and fuel combination, a full motel was on-site for the convenience of motorists and truckers. It is shown here as it existed in about 1968.

The Davis and Son Terminal and Restaurant opened in 1956 on U.S. 301 at Stony Creek, Virginia. Shortly thereafter, the construction of Interstate 95 placed the location on one of the East Coast's main north-south highways. This shot dates from the early 1960s. Today, an expanded travel center operates at this location, and a companion facility is located on Interstate 85 at Warfield, Virginia.

Bob Bartley's One Stop Truck Stop was a repairs-oriented facility, with the only indication of food service being the Tastee Freez in the background. Located just off of Highway 80 in Marshall, Texas, this truck stop advertised itself as selling two grades of diesel fuel, as well as gasoline, butane for refrigeration equipment, and all major brands of oils and additives. Public scales were available, as was truck washing. It is shown here as it appeared in about 1957.

J and L Oil Company developed the Tiki Oasis as a truck and travel stop on Interstate 80 at U.S. 51 in LaSalle/Peru, Illinois. Instead of bunk rooms, a complete motel was offered. It is seen here as it existed in about 1970.

Members of the Lewis family have been involved in petroleum marketing and automotive endeavors in southern West Virginia for much of the twentieth century. One of the operations was Lewis Terminal, a Keystone branded truck stop and café in Beckley, West Virginia. During the 1940s when this photograph was taken, the location was selling Elk Refining Co's. Keystone products.

Wide-open lots and expansive parking were two of the features that truck stops used to attract business. This location, operated by Marine Oil Co. on the Highway 45-51 bypass around Fulton, Kentucky, is an excellent example of this type of layout. Fuel islands scattered across the lot allowed for multiple truck fueling. The only other apparent attraction was a small café at the rear of the lot. This photo dates from 1961.

Sing Oil Company, based in Thomasville, Georgia, operated gas stations in small towns throughout Georgia and in the eastern parts of North and South Carolina. They also operated several locations they considered to be truck stops, including this location in Sylvester, Georgia. Apparently the inclusion of a diesel fuel pump at the side of this otherwise typical station makes the location into a truck stop by the company's standards. It was photographed in about 1950.

Sioux Oil Co. operated a truck stop and restaurant in the company's hometown of Newcastle, Wyoming. It was photographed here in about 1960.

Blue Ridge Oil Company of Hickory, North Carolina, operator of the Smile gas stations across western North Carolina, operated a truck stop along U.S. 19 and 23 just west of Asheville, North Carolina. It was photographed here in about 1959.

Southland Oil Co. was based in Savannah, Georgia, and began retail gasoline sales in 1956. The AAA Truck Center was located just outside of Savannah and was selling Southland's SOC products when photographed here in about 1965.

Jack and Navida Guinn operated Guinn's Super T Truck Stop, on U.S. 27 just north of Haynes City, Florida. Amenities included paved parking, bunks and showers, 24-hour mechanical and wrecker service, truck washing and, of course, the best home cookin' that a simple café could offer. Fuel sold here was supplied by Tampa-based private brander SuperTest. The station was photographed here about 1962.

Welco Truckers Lodge was a truck stop located on U.S. 6 at the southeast end of Walkerton, Indiana. Elaborate signage was designed to attract passing truckers and motorists, and it appears that the building-length signs were well illuminated for nighttime trade. Sources indicate that there were other Welco truck stops in the Chicagoland area in the 1950s and 1960s, but it is unknown if these sites are tied to this facility, which survived until relatively recent times. This photo dates from about 1952.

TRUCK STOP OPERATORS

Blue & White Service, Inc.

• Founded by Harold "Hap" Cloud on April 20, 1932 when he purchased a former Greyhound Bus Depot on Highway 52 in Andersonville, Indiana, which consisted of a 12-stool lunch counter and two hand-operated gas pumps.

• Hap kept the Greyhound blue and white color scheme. The depot was named, "The Blue & White Inn," and the name was retained during the ensuing expansion of the brand.

• Operating expenses at the time of acquisition of the depot were covered by $50.00 for food supplies and 200 gallons of gasoline.

• The original Blue & White Inn location was abandoned as a headquarters in 1943, and a second headquarters (also on Highway 52, nearer to Indianapolis) was procured.

• Name was changed to "Blue & White Service, Inc." in 1949.

• During the '50s, Blue & White operated a 24-hour wrecker truck service that had authorization in 26 states, as well as a fleet of 32 tire service trucks.

• Hap ran the business until the about 1985, when it was taken over by son Mike.

• The coming of I-65 in the 1960s, which routed traffic around the Indianapolis downtown core, helped to kill off the Blue & White truck stops in that area, all of which were sited along two-lane highways.

• Hap Cloud died in December, 1990. Following his death, the earliest gas stations and truck stops in the chain began to close.

• As late as 1994, Blue & White still operated a travel plaza/truck stop about 50 miles west of Indianapolis on I-70.

• The last day of operation of any Blue & White outlet was February 22, 2002.

• *Number of confirmed Blue & White branded truck stops operating in the U.S.:* Operated a total of 11 truck stops, all in Indianapolis and surrounding areas until approximately 1971. A single truck stop/travel plaza operated until 1994.

Pilot Oil Co. was founded with a single station located in Weber City, Virginia, in 1958, and for many years operated discount service stations throughout Virginia, Tennessee, West Virginia, and surrounding states. In 1981, Pilot opened its first travel plaza and in the 30-plus years that followed, built the organization into the single largest truck stop operator in the United States. This location is a contemporary photo of their location at White Pine, Tennessee.

Pilot Corp.

• Founded by James Haslam II in 1958 in Weber City, Virginia, as a single family-run gas station.

• Haslam had formerly been associated with LaFollette, Tennessee-based Fleet Oil. Early Pilot stations followed the formula developed by Fleet, with high volume discount stations located along well-traveled sections of highway leading into towns. Other early locations include stations in Roanoke, Galax, and Pearisburg, Virginia; Princeton, West Virginia; and throughout upper-east Tennessee.

• Marathon Oil Co. acquired half of Pilot's assets in 1965; in 1988, the Haslam Family bought back Marathon's interests.

• Pilot opened their first travel center in 1981.

• Formed a joint venture with Marathon Ashland Petroleum Co. (MAPCO) on March 15, 2001, and began operations on September 01, 2001. This resulted in a new name—Pilot Travel Centers (PTC)—that took effect on September 1, 2001, with PTC and Marathon both owning 50 percent interests. Press releases at that time indicated a projected increase to 235 locations within a few years. On October 01, 2008, PTC purchased Marathon's 50 percent stake in the joint venture and immediately sold the bulk of it to CVC Capital Partners, an international private equity firm.

• In February of 2003 Pilot acquired Williams Travel Centers.

• Pilot has always concentrated on truck traffic, and tends to have outlets that are more likely to represent a classic-style truck stop, rather than a typical travel plaza.

• Pilot sells approximately 10 percent of all diesel fuel in the U.S., making it the largest supplier of fuels to the trucking industry. Marathon remains as one of Pilot's main fuel suppliers after the sale of its share to CVC.

• After industry competitor Flying J experienced a series of financial difficulties, Pilot Oil purchased most of the Flying J operation in 2009. The Flying J brand name has currently been retained.

• *Number of confirmed Pilot branded truck stops operating in the U.S.:* In 2008, Pilot was operating more than 300 travel centers in approximately 40 states.

During the 1990s, Flying J partnered with CONOCO to put CONOCO branded fuels into Flying J truck stops nationwide. The arrangement lasted about 10 years, and put the CONOCO brand in states far from their traditional marketing area. This location is at Haw River, North Carolina, and was photographed in about 1998.

Flying J

• Osborne Jay Call (born 1917) operated a smattering of gas stations and automotive dealerships in Idaho, Utah, and Wyoming during and after the Great Depression.

• In his early years Jay's brother Reuel was a jobber for the Sinclair Oil Co., for an area in the western U.S. that bordered on Yellowstone National Park in the north, to the Four Corners area in the south.

• Reuel married into the Covey family, who later opened several Little America truck stops/motor lodges.

• Jay Call, son of Osborn Jay Call, was born in 1940.

• Jay's first gas station experience after high school came about when he managed "Jay's CutRate;" a gas station in Jackson, Wyoming, owned by his father. He later managed his first "Maverik" branded gas station in Willard, Utah, in 1960.

• Jay Call expanded the "Maverik" name in the early 1960s, on a collection of 19 gas stations, most of which were located in Idaho. No Maverik branded truck stops are known to have existed.

• The current Flying J corporation came into being in 1968, when Jay Call incorporated as Flying J, Inc. The name came from his love of flying airplanes. He re-named the four gas stations he was operating at that time to "Fastway."

• Flying J entered the truck stop business in 1979 with a 15 acre site near Ogden, Utah. It featured eight fueling islands and 29 fueling dispensers, with 23 dispensing diesel fuel. Also included were a Convenience Store, a recreation room, a 240-seat restaurant, and an 80-unit motel.

• In 1984, Flying J purchased the entire U.S. Husky Oil Co. branded retail operations, including a host of truck stops located in the northern Rocky Mountain states.

• Flying J entered a joint venture with CONCOCO on February 01, 1991, and CONOCO became Flying J's primary supplier of gasolines and diesel fuels. Flying J's demand for fuels quickly outpaced CONOCO's ability to supply, so an adjunct supply agreement and co-branding arrangement with the Shell Oil Co. was instituted in 2002.

• As of 2002, Flying J lead the U.S. in on-highway diesel fuel sales, operating nearly 160 full-service travel plazas in all states except Minnesota and six small New England states. At that time, Flying J ranked 45th on *Forbes* list of the largest U.S. private corporations, with annual sales exceeding $4.7 billion.

• Jay Call and corporate board member Richard E. "Buzz" Germer and Germer's wife were killed in the crash of a plane that Jay was piloting on March 15, 2005, five miles south of Hailey, Idaho.

• After a series of financial difficulties, Pilot Corp. purchased most of the Flying J operation in 2009. It has been announced that the Flying J brand would be retained.

• *Number of confirmed Flying J branded truck stops operating in the U.S.:* As of 2008, Flying J operated travel stops in 41 states and 6 Canadian provinces.

Pylon signage and illuminated arched entrance are hallmarks of today's T/A design. This facility was built as a T/A truck stop in the 1990s and originally included a Burger King, a Country Pride Restaurant, a BP gasoline station with T/A diesel islands, and a Days Inn "Daystop" motel. It is shown here in 2011, and is located on Interstate 40 just east of Greensboro, North Carolina. *Jason Henderson photo*

A different perspective shows the scale of the modern travel plaza. This T/A is located on Interstate 40 just east of Greensboro, North Carolina. *Jason Henderson photo*

TravelCenters of America

- The two original Truckstops of America locations, Roanoke (Troutville), Virginia, and Rochester, New York, were opened in the mid-1960s.
- In 1972, when the chain had grown to six stops, the operation was reorganized and incorporated as Truckstops of America by Phil Saunders.
- The two original Roanoke and Rochester locations were augmented by the addition of four more. These additional four were sited in Ashland, Virginia; Binghamton, New York; Mahway, New Jersey; and Caumbia, New York.
- The company was sold to Ryder, who later sold it to Standard Oil Co. of Ohio (SOHIO) in 1984.
- British Petroleum (BP) purchased the chain in 1987, then sold it to the Clipper Group in 1993.
- The Clipper Group combined the chain with National Auto/Truck Stops in 1997, adding 122 locations to the total. At that time, the name was changed to TravelCenters of America (T/A).
- At the time of the merger, National had twice as many outlets as T/A, most of which were former UNION 76 truck stops.
- T/A was the first corporation to bring fast food to truck stops, initially with a Burger King outlet in the early 1980s.

- In 1998, T/A acquired 17 Burns Bros. Travel Stops.
- In 1999, T/A merged with TravelPorts of America.
- *Number of confirmed T/A branded truck stops operating in the U.S.:* Currently operates more than 165 outlets in 40 states, and is listed as 96th in the *Forbes* list of 500 largest private companies. Partially owned by Portland, Oregon-based Freightliner Trucks, a division of Diamler Trucks North America, LLC.

Petro Stopping Centers

- Founded in 1975 in El Paso, Texas, by Jack Cardwell.
- As of early 2001, was operating or franchising more than 50 travel plazas in 30 states.
- Acquired by TravelCenters of America (T/A) on May 31, 2007. Prior to this acquisition, Volvo Trucks North America had owned 29% of Petro stock; Mobil Oil was a smaller minority owner.
- *Number of confirmed Petro branded truck stops operating in the U.S.:* At the time of the T/A acquisition, Petro was operating 69 travel centers in 33 states. Thomas M. O'Brien, President and CEO of T/A, stated that the two brands would continue to be operated as separate entities.

Love's Travel Plazas originated in Oklahoma and are well known in the south central portions of the country, but in recent years they have expanded coast-to-coast. This is an example of a design they have used in construction in the southeastern U.S. since the about 2005. It is located on Interstate 40 at Marion, North Carolina.

Love's

• Love's was founded in 1964 when Tom and Judy Love established Musket Corporation and leased a single conventional service station in Watonga, Oklahoma, selling Kerr McGee's Deep Rock gasoline.

• By 1972, when the Love's converted one of their locations to the company's first Convenience Store, they were operating some 40 sites. With the success of the first Convenience Store conversion, the company began converting all of their existing conventional stations to stores, choosing Love's Country Stores as their brand identification.

• By 1978, there were more than 60 Love's locations, scattered throughout Oklahoma, Kansas, Texas, New Mexico, and Colorado.

• In 1981 Love's opened their first Love's Travel Stop in Amarillo, Texas, a larger format location that combined the best of their Convenience Stores with the familiar truck stop concept. They would continue to build Love's Travel Stop locations, and in 1993 incorporated branded fast food facilities into their locations.

• Today, Love's is one of the fastest growing truck stop operators in the U.S., with more than 265 locations in 40 states.

Sapp Brothers

• The Sapp Brothers Truck Stop chain was founded with a single stop in Omaha, Nebraska, in 1971.

• In 1978, a new location was built on I-29 in Council Bluffs, Iowa.

• Other locations followed, including: Fremont, Nebraska (1982, rebuilt 1996); Cheyenne, Wyoming (1983); Odessa, Nebraska (1984); Commerce City, Colorado (1986); Columbus, Nebraska (1987); Peru, Illinois (1988); and three new Nebraska locations in 1989 at York, Ogallala, and Sidney.

• In the 1990s, expansion continued east and west: Salt Lake City, Utah in 1994; Clearfield, Pennsylvania, in 1996; and in Junction City, Kansas, in 1999.

• A location was added at Percival, Iowa, in 2001 to accommodate travel along a new bypass around Omaha and Council Bluffs.

• Sixteen locations are operating today, with locations in eight states.

Wilco

A. T. Williams Oil Company was founded in 1963 in Winston-Salem, North Carolina, when Arthur Tab Williams took over operation of seven Etna branded service stations previously owned and operated by his father-in-law, Roby Taylor. For the next 25 years, the company built up the Wilco brand in North Carolina and Virginia with a chain of discount service stations. In 1988, construction began on a new Wilco facility in Suffolk, Virginia, that was their first to include diesel fuel islands specifically designed for trucks. The success of that first effort fueled the implementation of a full-service truck stop. In 1990, Wilco opened their first such facility, located on Interstate 81 at Raphine, Virginia. Today, Wilco operates 31 truck stop facilities in seven states.

The A. T. Williams Oil Co. began operations in 1963, operating seven gas stations that had previously been operated by A. T. William's father-in-law, noted North Carolina discounter Roby Taylor. From that humble beginning the Wilco brand grew at a steady pace, and in 1988, the Williams team built their first truck stop in Suffolk, Virginia. Today Wilco operates hundreds of Hess branded outlets from Pennsylvania to Alabama, with a special emphasis on travel plazas. Shown here is one of their flagship travel plazas, in Myrtle Beach, South Carolina.

Wilco's marketing outside of North and South Carolina, and Virginia has been concentrated in the construction of travel plazas. Shown here is one of their earliest locations outside their concentrated marketing area, and is located at White Pine, Tennessee. This photo dates from 2009.

A typical modern Wilco travel plaza, with Hess branded fuels and a Stuckey's Convenience Store, a Dairy Queen and a Wendy's franchise. It is located in along Interstate 77 at Winnsboro, South Carolina, and was photographed in 2009.

Chapter 4
TRAVEL STOP OPERATORS

Stuckey's

• The original tourist-oriented travel stop chain. Stuckey's was founded in Eastman, Georgia, in 1936 by William Stuckey, who had expanded a pecan buying operation into a successful roadside stand selling pecans and candies.

• Prior to WWII, Stuckey's was operating locations in Unadilla and Folkston, Georgia, and Hilliard, Florida. After the war, further expansion was made in Georgia and Florida, with new locations added in Virginia (Petersburg, 1949); South Carolina (Aiken, 1950); Tennessee (Cleveland, LaFollette and Rockwood, 1950); Mississippi (Toomsuba, 1951); North Carolina (Smithfield 1952); Alabama (Loxley 1952); and Kentucky (Georgetown, 1952) rounding out their presence throughout the southeastern U.S. At the close of 1955, Stuckey's was operating 41 locations, with various gasoline brands being sold sold.

• In the latter half of the 1950s, the chain further expanded, standardizing on TEXACO gasoline where available. Locations eventually expanded to create a coast-to-coast chain.

• Stuckey's went through a series of ownership changes, which, in 1967, ended in the chain being in the hands of nationwide dairy operator Pet Corp.

• The gasoline shortages of the 1970s, combined with disinterest on the parts of the new ownership, forced many Stuckey's locations to close. The surviving operations were purchased back by the Stuckey family in 1985. Today, a few of the original locations survive, and numerous traditional Convenience Stores operate as franchised Stuckey's candy dealers.

Truck Stop Operations

• Stuckey's locations never functioned as truck stops, per se, but their business model served as a prototype for the automotive side of today's travel plazas.

Stuckey's was the original chain-operated tourist stop. Based on prior experience with the local southern Georgia pecan crop, William Stuckey began selling pecans at retail through a simple roadside stand. This led to the first Stuckey's, which opened in 1937 in Eastman, Georgia. That location is shown here, as it appeared in the early post-WWII era.

Stuckey's second location opened in Unadilla, Georgia, in 1939. It is seen here in about 1948.

Due to their locations along major highways, many Stuckey's outlets became de facto truck stops, although they were intended to be oriented towards tourists. Location #19 opened in Smithfield, North Carolina, in 1951.

By the early 1960s, Stuckeys' designs had become standardized, and all new stores were constructed in a style similar to this location, on U.S. 1 just south of Bunnell, Florida. This shot is from about 1962.

One of the main north-south tourist routes to and from Florida was U.S. 301. Many truck stops and tourist stops were located along the highway in the vicinity of Jesup, Georgia, and it was there that Stuckey's opened their 35th location, in 1955. It is shown here at about the time it opened.

Stuckeys #12, Tallulah Falls, Georgia, opened in 1950. It is seen here about 1955, when it served as the entrance to Tallulah Gorge Park.

As Stuckey's began what turned out to be a nationwide expansion, several early stores were located in Indiana. This location, at Centerville, Indiana, was built in a style similar to the standardized units of the early 1960s. Phillips 66 products were sold at this location, because the Stuckey's-preferred TEXACO brand was not locally available.

Stuckeys #11 opened in Yulee, Florida, in 1950. After WWII, America discovered the glory of the open highway and families took to the roads in record numbers. Florida was a popular vacation destination, and in Florida in the 1950s there was always a Stuckey's nearby. This photo dates from 1955.

One of the earliest locations in Stuckey's northern expansion was this site at Nortonsville, Kentucky. It opened in about 1954 in an existing building, as is shown here in a photo from about that time.

Horne's was founded in Bayard, Florida, in 1949 when Bob Horne, who had worked for Stuckey's in various capacities, turned his family's "Horne's Beautyrest Cabins" motor court into a tourist stop. It featured restaurant facilities, a gas station, and a tourist store. This photo shows the location in the early 1950s.

Another classic old Stuckey's location, store #16 in Acworth, Georgia. In the years before Stuckey's developed their own architectural style, they utilized existing structures. This location is seen as it appeared in 1954.

Horne's

• Horne's was founded in Bayard, Florida, in 1949 when Bob Horne, who had previously worked for the Stuckey's corporation in various capacities, turned his family's Horne's Beautyrest Cabins Motor Court into a tourist stop, complete with restaurant facilities, a gas station, and a tourist store.

• During the 1950s, Horne's built some distinctive tourist stops, each featuring a bright yellow roof that could be seen from a distance along the two-lane. Each location sold gasoline, with the brand varying by location, and as the chain grew, each location also began to feature a full sit-down restaurant, which was distinctly different from Stuckey's snack bar or lunch counter-type facilities.

• By the 1960s, some key Horne's locations were adding motels to their tourist stops.

• As the Interstate Highway System grew, Horne's locations were often bypassed and by the 1970s, the chain was withdrawing from many areas. Their motel business, however, would survive into the 21st century, and at least one franchise operator, at Port Royal, Virginia, continues to operate a Horne's Restaurant and store.

Stuckey's first Florida location, store #3, opened in 1941 in Hilliard, Florida. It is seen here as it appeared in about 1955. Sinclair products were being sold at that time.

In the mid-1950s, Horne's settled on a standardized design for their stops that featured a highly visible yellow roof. Horne's locations included full restaurants, a stark contrast to the usual Stuckey's snack bars. Locations based on this design were built throughout the United States and in eastern Canada, and, with the many amenities available at each location, easily became, in essence, stopping places for many road-weary truckers.

Nickerson Farms

• Tourist-oriented travel stop operation similar in design and execution to Stuckey's (the originator of the travel stop category). Some outlets doubled as ersatz truck stops due to their sites being conveniently located along Interstates; their close affiliation with the Skelly Oil Co. and its branded truck stop program; and the availability of a full-service restaurant and expansive parking areas. No showering or sleeping facilities were provided for drivers.

• The first Nickerson Farms outlet was a converted Witmor Farms site located in Oklahoma on I-44 at the Buckhorn exit.

• *Number of confirmed Nickerson Farms branded, Skelly-supplied locations operating in the U.S.:*

1966, Skelly and Nickerson Farms agreed to open co-branded facilities at 70 Interstate Highway locations in 17 states.

1967: 21 Nickerson Farms/Skelly co-branded outlets were in operation in eight states.

1977: approximately 65 Nickerson Farms outlets were listed as operating in seven states.

• The Nickerson Farms chain ceased to exist in about 1980.

Many of the early roadside establishments intended mostly for motorists also served as de facto truck stops. Early incarnations were located on rural two-lanes; later versions tended to be sited on rural Interstates. The most ubiquitous of these sub-types were Stuckey's and Horne's. A later entry into this non-traditional truck stop genre was Nickerson Farms. In 1966, all Nickerson Farms locations were converted to one fuel supplier, Skelly Oil Co., thus strengthening a tie between this non-traditional truck stop sub-type, and the operator of the second-largest truck stop chain in America. By 1967, the program was gaining ground, with 21 Nickerson Farms/Skelly combinations in operation in eight midwestern states. All Nickerson Farms outlets featured a signature red-tiled roof, topping pseudo-English Tudor style architecture. The company ceased to exist in about 1980. Nickerson Farms operated 70 gasoline/restaurant locations in 17 midwestern and western states, at their peak.

Chapter 5

TRUCK STOP ADVERTISING

CHAMPLIN TRUCK STOP

I-40 & Hwy. 64 Interchange

Sallisaw, Okla.

Restaurant — Trucker's Lounge — Showers
24-Hour Service

Manager:
Ed Stites

Telephone:
(918) 775-4686

Ed Stites' Stites Oil Co. operated this Champlin truck stop located just off I-40 at the Highway 64 Interchange in Sallisaw, Oklahoma. This 1970 NTS Truck Stop advertisement depicts the Champlin Truck Stop as it appeared in probably about the mid-1960s. Note the usage of a few "Googie" architectural conventions: an acutely angled, "folded" pump island canopy, and a cornice announcing "Restaurant" and "Champlin" that is angled downward, towards the road.

El Paso
TRUCK TERMINAL

Interstate 10 & Airway Blvd.
**6666 GATEWAY EAST
EL PASO, TEXAS**

Phone: (915) 772-1441

Providing Complete Service . . . .

Every time you stop you get all the modern services, up-to-date facilities and old-fashion Texas hospitality you expect and deserve

EXCELLENT
24-Hour Restaurant Specializing in Service

"Stop in and see us soon."

For The Driver:
- MOTEL – 20 Units
  Single or Double
- FAX WESTERN UNION FLV
- Complete "GENERAL STORE"
- BARBER SHOP
- SHOWERS
- DRIVERS LOUNGE
  Air-Conditioned

For The Truck
- THERMO KING
  Dealership and Service
  24 Hour Call
- RPM DELCO PRODUCTS
- MINOR REPAIR SHOP
- TRUCK WASHING
- STEAM CLEANING
- AXLE SCALES

easy on–easy off INTERSTATE 10 CHEVRON

FINA — 20 Miles North of Houston, Texas — FINA

"EASY ON AND OFF – BOTH WAYS"
INTERSTATE 45 AT RICHEY ROAD
20 MILES NORTH OF HOUSTON

LARGE
PARKING AREA
3½ ACRES PAVED

All approved credit cards accepted

FOOD

OPEN 24 HOURS
EMERGENCY TRUCK SERVICE
PLENTY OF SLEEPING AREA FOR TIRED TRUCKERS

Ultra modern restaurant seating 80 people. Open 24 hours.

FUEL

Flats Fixed Anytime ROAD SERVICE Phone: 713/ 444-7389

Another expansive Third Generation truck stop, this one branded FINA, was located 20 miles north of Houston on I-45. This Texas-size truck stop offered 3.5 acres of paved parking, a restaurant seating 80 people, and fuels costing right around 30 cents per gallon. Trucks fueled at left, or under the overhead canopy at center; autos fueled under several islands under their own canopy at right. Between the two fueling areas was a restaurant, behind which was the diesel truck servicing building. A credit card exchange program allowed truckers to use any major oil company credit card on premises.

The El Paso Truck Terminal was one of the largest in the Southwest. Featuring Chevron and Standard Oil Co. products, the stop also boasted of a 20-unit motel; a complete "General Store;" a barber shop; and an air-conditioned drivers' lounge. A smiling waitress was always on hand to deliver drivers a steaming hot cup of coffee. A couple of interesting typos show up here, highlighting the naiveté of the copyeditors of the time: Chevron has always marketed "RPM DELO" products. This ad shows them marketing "AC DELCO" products (DELCO has always been a division of General Motors). The ad also expounds that, "Every time you stop, you get all the modern services, up-to-date facilities and old-fashion Texas hospitality you expect and deserve." In correct English, shouldn't that be, "old-fashioned?"

GARRETT'S Midway Truck Stop

Acclaimed by OVERDRIVE For Having *'the smoothest and strongest truck parking lot in the world.'* It's ALL CONCRETE, *of course!*

RESTAURANT-- Buffet lunch on Sunday   **BUNKS**   Phone: 583-2493

Wood River, Nebraska *On I-80, 30 Miles East Of Kearney*

Overdrive truckers' magazine proclaimed Garrett's Midway Truck Stop (T-211) in Wood River, Nebraska, operated by Warren Garrett, as having the "Smoothest and strongest truck parking lot in the world" in this 1968 ad. Here, a pair of Macks—an early 1950s B-61 conventional (left), and mid-1960s cabover (right)—take on fuel, while sitting on that superlative concrete slab. The, "It's All Concrete, of course!" tag line makes it appear as though the whole ad was paid for by a Nebraska concrete promotion association, instead of it being a reference to the fact that it's not graveled, as earlier, less-advanced truck stop facilities had been.

In the mid to late 1960s, San Antonio's "Gas & Eat" Truck Stop featured TEXACO fuels, a "Modern Restaurant," "6 Acres of Paved Parking," and "TV Lounge and Sleeping Rooms." The gigantic roadside neon signage undoubtedly pulled 'em in off both I-35 (I-H 35, according to the ad) and Highway 81. Note the curved fuel island canopy that allows for autos to fuel nearest the fuel building, then bends upward nearer the road to allow for trucks to fuel at the same island. The Emeryville cabover at far left displays an odd twin steering axle setup.

GAS & EAT TRUCK STOP

I-H 35 and O'Connor Road
SAN ANTONIO, TEXAS

TEXACO

NTS — NATIONAL TRUCKERS SERVICE

★ MODERN RESTAURANT

TV LOUNGE and SLEEPING ROOMS

★ WESTERN UNION — FBR

★ 6 ACRES PAVED PARKING

★ WASH & LUBE BAYS

Mail: 6103 Hwy. 81 North   **Phone : 512/ 655-1251**

Holden Truck Center

Freeway 99, Just North of 24th Street (Route 58)

C. D. "Slim" Holden & Euel Largent

Bakersfield, California

24 HOUR RESTAURANT•TRUCK REPAIR •THERMO–KING AGENT
WASH AND STEAM • BARBER SHOP • INSIDE 70' LUBE PIT •70'
SCALE • PROPANE • SHOWERS • TICKET PRINTER PUMPS
LIQUID NITROGEN • BUNK HOUSE • BLOWER AND BUNKER ICE
WESTERN UNION • CLOTHES AND ACCESSORIES

TEXACO   NTS

3775 Pierce Road, Bakersfield, California 93308   Phone: 327-5781

Sometimes a line drawing can convey as much as a photo without sacrificing any visual appeal; thus may be the case with C. D. "Slim" Holden and Euel Largent's Holden Truck Center located on historic border-to-border Highway 99 in Bakersfield, California. Obviously taken from a photo, this attractive ad displays a three-bay "Diesel Truck Repair" center, an expansive array of tires in front of a large "Tire Service" area, and a multi-lane fuel island area, sans canopy. Although this ad was published in the late '60s, the pickup truck near lower center appears to be of a vintage 15 years earlier; the truck at bottom right appears to be from perhaps the late 1930s. The mock oil tower alludes to Barkersfield's earlier-century ties with the extensive oil fields in the region. An expansive list of amenities ties the whole piece together.

IOWA 80 STANDARD TRUCK STOP

On Interstate 80 At Walcott Jct.
WALCOTT, IOWA   Phone 319 284-6666

L.P. Gas
Wrecker Service
Lube and Oil Changes
Regular - - Ethyl
Premiere Diesel
Axle Scales

Steam Cleaning
Western Union
Showers
Air Conditioned Bunks
T.V. Lounge
Restaurant

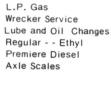

Wrecker Service

The "World's Largest Truck Stop" wasn't always. At the time that this modest 1968 *Overdrive* magazine ad appeared there was no mention of Iowa 80's size. However, at only about four years of age, Iowa 80 would still have to concede Little America in Wyoming as being the world's largest gas station/truck stop. However, the ad does mention a long list of services not necessarily available at other truck stops of the era, including steam cleaning, a TV lounge, air-conditioned bunks, and "Premiere Diesel." The Third Generation truck stop was being born.

LARRY'S TRUCK STOP

U.S. 20, INTERSTATE 90 — ON THE NEW YORK STATE LINE
NORTH EAST, PA.

Complete Truck Stop Service

A NATIONAL   TRUCK STOP

We Service A Specialized Group

The Trucking Industry

Your Satisfaction Adds Up To

2 *Mighty Important Things*
to us!

YOUR CONTINUED PATRONAGE
and
MORE BUSINESS

Larry's Truck Stop was a Fleetwing outlet located on the New York state line, at North East, Pennsylvania. Neon signage adorns this rural truck stop; note that the "Larry's--Fuel--Eat--Rest" signage is augmented with tracer-light arrows. There's a Freightliner facing the camera at right; further right is an additional Fleet-Wing roadside sign near the road.

KEY OIL COMPANY TRUCK STOPS

CHANNELVIEW, TEXAS
16 Miles East of Houston
Interstate 10 — Magnolia Exit

SEALY, TEXAS
54 Miles West of Houston
Interstate 10 — Pyka Road Exit

Phone: (713) 452-1043   •   FREE! Sauna Baths & Showers   •   Phone: (713) 885-3519

| Color TV Lounge
Air Conditioned Cafe
Road Service Western Union
Lube, Wash, Oil-Change Services
Clothes Washer & Dryer | PRIVATE, AIR CONDITIONED
BUNK ROOMS AND TILE SHOWERS
•
N. T. S. CREDIT CARDS HONORED | Top Grade Gasoline
Highest Cetane Diesel
Paved Parking Area
Drive through Bays
Clothing |

The Key Oil Co. operated two branded truck stops, both in Texas; one in Channelview, and the other in Sealy. What makes this ad interesting is the "quaint" hand-drawn KEY logo at center, as well as the photos. Both locations offer canopied fueling islands. The advertised "sauna baths" are one of the out-of-the-ordinary truck stop offerings for the time. The "Highest Cetane Diesel" claim may be specious, as all diesel fuel at that time was of equal cetane rating. In the right-hand photograph, an F-Model Mack cabover gets attention from an employee on a ladder; next door, a GMC 5000-series truck and trailer combination takes on some of that "highest cetane" fuel.

The August, 1968 issue of *Overdrive* magazine offered this photo of Les Fuller's Truck Town, Inc. (T-176) taken at an angle that was opposite from that which was offered in the 1966 through 1980-'81 Skelly Truck Stop Directories. Here we can see that the Skelly diamond signage on the Les Fuller billboard has been moved to a spot closer to roadside; a mid-1960s GMC Crackerbox cabover sites directly beneath. There appears to be an asphalt entranceway off the main highway, but it fizzles out about 40 feet in, and no other paving can be accessed until the fuel islands are reached. The ad states that Truck Town is located "Exactly half way across Texas." Whomever painted the distorted Skelly signage on the side of the truck service building has a lot of audacity calling himself a sign painter...

Woody's two Skelly New Mexico Truck Stops (T-141 and T-219) were featured in this advertisement in a mid-1960s *Overdrive* magazine. The Roswell location is depicted from an angle that is almost opposite from the shot that is featured in the Skelly Truck Stop Directories of the era. At left, signage advertises Diesel for 19.9 cents/gal.; at right, Regular gasoline is advertised for 24.9 cents/gal.

Located at Exit 16 on the Ohio Turnpike, Mike & Vic's AMOCO Truck Service offers truckers an extensive array of services that goes well beyond what other truck stops were offering at the date of this ad's publication in 1965: two grades of diesel fuel; CO2 chill blasting for produce and other perishable loads; welding services; cattle pens for temporary offloading of livestock; "Rabbi Services;" a courtesy car for transport to neighboring businesses; physician and dental services; Notary Public services; a laundromat; and a barber shop. This shot depicts Mike & Vic's concrete fuel islands still surrounded by graveled approaches. A Brockway cabover can be seen at far left, while a cabover Kenworth fuels at far right. Mohawk 10:00-series truck tires are advertised for $69.00 each in the window of the fuel office (today's equivalent would cost approximately $400.00 each). The massive rooftop AMOCO Truck Stop sign must have been a stunning sight to behold at night!

BIBLIOGRAPHY

ARTICLES
• Bly, Laura: *USA Today* newspaper; Friday, June 7, 1996; "Truck stops: No longer the pits."
• *Commercial Carrier Journal*; August, 2000: "Truck Stops: Forging a Partnership With Fleets."
• Dye, Tim: *Tiger Hightest Magazine*; #39, 1996: "The History of Hi-Speed of Toledo, Ohio."
• Henderson, Wayne: *Petroleum Collectibles Monthly Magazine*; Volume 1, No.8, August, 1995: "Diesel Fuel and 100 Mile Coffee."
• Henry, Lyell: *The Lincoln Highway Forum*; Volume 5, No. 1, Fall, 1997: "'One-Stops' on the Lincoln Highway: Four Midwestern Examples."
• *Illinois State Tollway Authority*; June 17, 2003: "Illinois Tollway Launches Comprehensive Oases Redevelopment Project."
• Kudlemyer, Guy: *Check The Oil!* magazine; October, 1998: "Skelly Truck Stops – Part 1."
• Kudlemyer, Guy: *Overdrive* magazine: "Trucker Turf: Skelly Oil catered to truckers with 1960s truck stops."
• Lucas, Kirsten: *Oregon Daily Journal of Commerce*; December 05, 1998: "Burns Bros. puts brakes on local shops."
• Ma, Earl: *Check The Oil!* magazine; "Petro-Glyph: You're Always Right With Blue & White (Parts 1 and 2)."
• O'Connor, John: *Family Sells Famous Route 66 Truck Stop* © 2003, The Associated Press.
• Phillips, Pete: *SCA Journal*; Spring, 2004: "Sign Lines."
• Raflo, Lisa; Durbin, Jeffrey: *Route 66 Magazine*; Spring, 2001: "Teal Roofs & Pecan Logs."
• Reid, Robert L.: *Civil Engineering Magazine*; June, 2006; "Special Report: The Interstate Highway System at 50; Paving America From Coast to Coast."
• *Road King Magazine*; July-August, 2000; "Iowa 80 TA Celebrates Truckers All Year."
• *Road King Magazine*; July-August, 2002; "Bunk Rooms and Gang Showers: Once the norm, they've given way to private facilities."
• *Road King Magazine*; July-August, 2002: "TA Turns 30."
• *Skelly News*; November-December, 1966: "Gay Johnson Country."
• *Skelly News*; May-June, 1968: "Black Hills Opens Skelly Truck Stop."
• *Skelly News*; November-December, 1966: "Interstate Truck Stop… Salina Truck Plaza on I-70."
• *Skelly News*; May-June, 1967: "In The News: The Holger Anderson Story."
• *Skelly News*; May-June, 1972: "Travelog."
• *Skelly News*; September-October, 1972: "A Special Report on the Skelly Fuel Stop at Edwards, Colorado: From Excavation to a Service Station."
• Teague, Tom: *Route 66 Magazine*; Fall, 2000; Winter, 2000/01 "Seventy-two & Still Truckin'"
• Toner, Mike: *The Legend*; Fall, 2003: "First Cross-Country Car Trip."
• *Trucker's Adviser, The*; June, 1965: "Wildwood: Another PURE Opening"

BOOKS
• Adams, Ron: *Big Rigs of the 1950s* © 2001; Motorbooks International – St. Paul, Minnesota.
• Adams, Ron: *Big Rigs of the 1960s* © 2004; Motorbooks International – St. Paul, Minnesota.
• Beck, Ken; Clark, Jim; Kerr, Les: *The All-American Truck Stop Cookbook* © 2002; Rutledge Hill Press—Nashville, Tennessee.
• Benjamin, Scott; Henderson, Wayne: *Gas Pump Globes* © 1993; Motorbooks International Publishers & Wholesalers—Osceola, Wisconsin.
• Carlisle, Howard M.: *The Flying J story: From Cut-Rate Stations to the Leader in Interstate Travel Plazas; An Authorized Biography and Company History* © 2002; HMC Publishing—Logan, Utah.
• Ewens, Graeme; Ellis, Michael: *The Cult of the Big Rigs and the Life of the Long Haul Trucker* © 1977; Chartwell Books, Inc.—Secaucus, New Jersey.
• Franzwa, Gregory M.: *The Lincoln Highway: Wyoming* © 1999; The Patrice Press—Tucson, Arizona.
• Heimann, Jim; *Car Hops and Curb Service: A History of American Drive-In Restaurants, 1920—1960* © 1996; Chronicle Books—San Francisco, California.
• Henderson, Wayne; Benjamin, Scott: *Gas Stations* © 1994; Motorbooks International Publishers & Wholesalers—Osceola, Wisconsin.
• Henderson, Wayne; Benjamin, Scott: *Guide to Gasoline Logos* © 1997; PCM Publishing—LaGrange, Ohio.
• Heavy Duty Trucking Magazine: *100 Years of Trucking* © 1998; Newport Communications Group—Skokie, Illinois.
• Heilig, John: *Mack: Driven for a Century* © 1999; Publications International, Ltd. – Lincolnwood, Illinois.
• Hess, Alan: *Googie: Fifties Coffee Shop Architecture* © 1985; Chronicle Books—San Francisco, California.

- Hokanson, Drake: *The Lincoln Highway: Main Street Across America* © 1988; University of Iowa Press, Iowa City, Iowa.
- Iowa 80 Group: *The Perfect Spot: Iowa 80's Journey From Iowa Cornfield to World's Largest Truckstop* © 2004; Iowa 80 Group—Walcott, Iowa.
- Ironside, Roberta Louise: *An Adventure Called Skelly* © 1970; Appleton-Century-Crofts, Meredith Corp.—New York, New York.
- Jakle, John A.; Sculle, Keith A.: *The Gas Station in America* © 1994; The Johns Hopkins University Press—Baltimore, Maryland.
- Jones, Vane A.; *North American Radio-TV Station Guide* © 1970; Howard W. Sams & Co., Inc.—Indianapolis, Indiana.
- Love, Ed; Drivas, Larry T.: *Gas and Oil Trademarks, Volume One* © 1988; Villa Publishing Syndicate—Colorado Springs, Colorado.
- Love, Ed: *Gas and Oil Trademarks, Volume Two* © 1990; Villa Publishing Syndicate—Colorado Springs, Colorado.
- Vieyra, Daniel I.: *Fill'er Up: An Architectural History of America's Gas Stations* © 1979; Macmillan Publishing Co, Inc.—New York, New York.
- Waddell, Paul R.; Niven, Robert F.: *Sign of the 76: The Fabulous Life and Times of the Union Oil Co. of California* © 1976, Union Oil Co. of California – Los Angeles, California.
- Wagner, James K.: *GMC Heavy Duty Trucks, 1927-1987* © 2004; Iconografix, Inc.—Hudson, Wisconsin.

INTERNET
- http://en.wikipedia.org/wiki/Nickerson_Farms
- http://en.wikipedia.org/wiki/Truck_stop
- http://www.archway.org/default.php
- http://www.cfsi.com/aboutus.html
- http://www.chevron.com/products/learning_center/history
- http://www.citgo.com/AboutCITGO/CITGOTimeline
- http://www.hornes.com
- http://www.illinoistollway.com/portal/page?_pageid=57,1300922,57_1301152&_dad=portal&_schema=PORTAL
- http://www.jubitz.com
- http://www.lincolnhighwayassoc.org
- http://www.littleamerica.com
- http://members.aol.com/sum41angel02/competitors/hornes/hornes.htm
- http://members.aol.com/sum41angel02/competitors/nickerson/nickfarms.htm
- http://www.natso.com
- http://www.ohioturnpike.org/history.html
- http://www.panix.com/~rbean/oasis
- http://www.petrotruckstops.com
- http://www.pilotcorp.com
- http://www.puremarketers.com
- http://p66conoco76.conocophillips.com/Our+Products/index.htm
- http://www.sinclairoil.com/html/body_about_sinclair
- http://www.texaco.com/texaco/abouttexaco/history.htm
- *The Torch and Oval;* AMOCO Online Magazine, © 1996.
- http://www.tshaonline.org/handbook/online/articles/DD/dod3.html

PERIODICALS
- *Check The Oil!* magazine; Three Fifty Six, Inc.; Powell, Ohio (various issues).
- *Petroleum Collectibles Monthly* magazine; Petroleum Collectibles Monthly, Inc.; LaGrange, Ohio (various issues).
- *Overdrive* magazine; Transamerican Press, Inc.; Los Angeles, California; Vol. 8, No.8, August, 1968
- *Overdrive* magazine; Transamerican Press, Inc.; Los Angeles, California; Vol. 9, No.5, May, 1969
- *Overdrive* magazine; Transamerican Press, Inc.; Los Angeles, California; Vol. 9, No.7, July, 1969
- *Overdrive* magazine; Transamerican Press, Inc.; Los Angeles, California; Vol. 9, No.10, October, 1969
- *Owner Operator* magazine; Chilton Co.; Radnor, Pennsylvania (various issues).
- *Route 66 Magazine;* Laughlin, Nevada; Williams, Arizona (various issues).
- *Wheels of Time* magazine; American Truck Historical Society; Kansas City, Missouri (various issues).
- *Tiger Hightest Magazine;* Garage Wall Graphics; Broken Arrow, Oklahoma (various issues).
- *Trucker's Adviser, The;* National Trucking Association; Auburn, New York; Vol. 6, #6, June, 1965.

PRESS RELEASES
• *Death of O. Jay Call;* Virginia Parker, Director of Marketing, Flying J. Corporation.

THESES
• Breitbach, Jessica: *A Home Away From Home: Telling The Story of the Trucking Industry Through the Preservation of 1960s Truck Stops.* © 2005.
• Rowcroft, Jessica: *The Truck Stop Industry in The United States* © 2001.

TRUCK STOP DIRECTORIES AND LISTS
• American/Standard/AMOCO: 1960; 1961; 1963; 1964-5; 1966; 1967; 1968; 1969; 1976; 1977. (Various publishers).
• Atlantic Richfield Company Truck Station Directory: May, 1970; Atlantic Richfield Co., Los Angeles, CA.
• DX Division Service Stations Selling Diesel Fuel: 1969; Mid Continent Petroleum Co., Tulsa, OK.
• Getty Truck Stop Directory: 1984; Getty Refining and Marketing Co., P.O. Box 1650, Tulsa, OK 74102.
• GULF Truck Stop Directory: 1962; Gulf Oil Corp., P.O. Box 1519, Houston, TX 77001.
• Husky International Directory Map: 1977; Cody, WY, 82414.
• Mid-Continent Truck Stop Guide: 1971; Mid Continent Oil Co., P.O. Box 1370, West Memphis, AR 72301.
• Mid-Continent U.S./Canada Truck Stop Directory: June, 1976; Mid Continent Oil Co., P.O. Box 1370, West Memphis, AR 72301.
• MOBIL Oil Corporation Retail Diesel Service Stations: Mid-late 1960s; Standard Oil Co. of New York, NY.
• National Association of Truck Stop Operators (NATSO) Membership Directory, April-May-June, 1971: NATSO, 501 Slaters Lane, Alexandria, Virginia, 22314
• National Auto/Truckstops, Inc. Access 76 Truckstop Directory: August 01, 1993.
• National Truck Stop Directory; 1995: TR Information Publishers, P.O. Box 476, Clearwater, FL, 34617.
• National Truckers Service, Inc. (NTS): January/February, 1970; Fall, 1975; National Truckers Service, Inc.; 6801 Calmont; P.O. Box 12247, Fort Worth, Texas 76116.
• NATSO (National Association of Truck Stop Operators) Travel Plazas and Truckstops Membership Directory: 1988; 1995; NATSO, Inc., P.O. Box 1285, 1199 N. Fairfax St., Suite 801, Alexandria, VA, 22314.
• Official Wire Service Points Directory: 1973; J.J. Keller & Associates, Inc., Neenah, Wisconsin.
• Phillips 66 Truck Stop Directory: May, 1970; Phillips Petroleum Co., Bartlesville, OK, 74004.
• PURE 1957 Truck Station Map: Rand/McNally, 1957.
• PURE 1963 Truck Station Map: Rand Mc/Nally, 1963.
• PURE Truck Stop Directories: 1958; 1960; 1961; 1962; 1963; 1965; 1966; 1967.
• PURE Truck Stop Directory Supplement: 1969; Rand/McNally, 1969.
• Shamrock Truck Stop Directory: April, 1969; Diamond Shamrock Oil and Gas Co., P.O. Box 631, Amarillo, TX 79105.
• Shell 1968 United States Truck Stop Map: 1968; Shell Oil Co., San Francisco, CA.
• Sinclair Truck Stop Guide: 1960; 1964; Sinclair Refining Co., 600 Fifth Ave., New York 20, NY.
• Sinclair Truck Stop Network brochure: June, 1998; Sinclair Oil Co., P.O. Box 30825, Salt Lake City, UT, 84130-1825
• Skelly Design Brochure: A Synopsis of the Pre-Engineered Buildings Offered By Skelly Oil Company. Skelly Oil Co., Box 436, Kansas City 41, Missouri.
• Skelly Truck Stop Directories: 1963; 1964/65; 1966; 1967; 1968; 1969; 1971/72; 1973/74/75; 1976/77; 1978/79; 1980/81. Skelly Oil Co., Box 436, Kansas City 41, Missouri.
• SUNOCO Division Service Stations Selling Diesel Oil: 1969; Sun Refining and Marketing Co., 1608 Walnut St., Philadelphia, PA 19103.
• TEXACO Truck Stop Guide: 1966; TEXACO, New York, NY.
• TEXACO Truck Service Centers Guide: 1969; TEXACO, New York, NY.
• TEXACO Truck Stop Directory: November 01,1991; 1994; TEXACO, P.O. Box 921002, Ft. Worth, TX 76121-0002.
• UNION 76 National Truck Stop Directory: 1976; 1978; 1981; Union Oil Co. of California, Truck Industry Sales Dept., 200 E. Golf Rd., Palatine, IL 60067.
• UNOCAL 76 National Truck Stop Directory: 1983; 1985; Union Oil Co. of California, Truck Industry Sales Dept., 1650 E. Golf Rd., Schaumburg, IL 60196.
• UNOCAL 76 National Auto/Truck Stop Directory: 1988; 1990; 1991; Union Oil Co. of California, Truck Industry Sales Dept., 1650 E. Golf Rd., Schaumburg, IL 60196.